The Episcopal Controversy Reviewed

Emory, John, Bp., 1789-1835, Emory, Robert, 1814-1848

THE

EPISCOPAL CONTROVERSY

REVIEWED.

BY JOHN EMORY, D D.

LATE ONE OF THE BISHOPS OF THE METHODIST EPISCOPAL CHURCH

EDITED BY HIS SON,

FROM AN UNFINISHED MANUSCRIPT.

NEW-YORK·

PUBLISHED BY T MASON AND G LANE,

FOR THE METHODIST EPISCOPAL CHURCH, AT THE CONFERENCE OFFICE,
200 MULBERRY-STREET

J Collord, Printer.
1838.

PREFACE TO EPISCOPAL CONTROVERSY,

BY THE EDITOR

The late period at which this work is presented to the public, and the unfinished state in which it appears, will be best explained by a brief statement of the circumstances attending its composition and publication About ten or twelve years since, when the economy of the Methodist Episcopal Church was assailed by foes from within, the author of the present essay undertook its defence in a tract entitled " A Defence of our Fathers, and of the original Organization of the Methodist Episcopal Church," &c. That work passed through several editions, and as the demand seemed likely to continue, the publishers requested the author to prepare a revised edition This he appears, at one time, to have contemplated, as a copy was found interleaved, apparently for that purpose Subsequently, however, he seems to have been satisfied, from his own observation and the opinion of others, that, inasmuch as the controversy which had elicited the original work was dying away, while the attacks upon the organization of the church, both openly and secretly, were perhaps increasing in other quarters, it would be better to prepare an entirely new work, in which the government of the Methodist Episcopal Church should be defended, not merely against the cavils of a particular party or sect, but against all opposition , and its entire accordance with Scriptural authority and primitive usage be established by a full investigation of the subject of episcopacy in general. and of Methodist episcopacy in particular Such was the plan of the present work: the sudden death of the author left it but partially and imperfectly executed The manuscript contained only a discus-

sion of the subject of episcopacy in general, in a reply
to "An Essay on the Invalidity of Presbyterian Ordination, by John Esten Cooke, M D ," and a part of a reply
to a tract entitled "Episcopacy tested by Scripture," by
Dr H U. Onderdonk, then assistant bishop of Pennsylvania.   Whether it was intended to notice any other
works on the opposite side, may be doubted, as the
first afforded an opportunity to examine the argument
from the Fathers, the second the argument from Scripture.   Why an answer to these two works, one of
which was published in 1829, and the other in 1830,
was delayed until 1835, the year of the author's death,
none will inquire who have any knowledge of his ardu-
ous and incessant engagements, first, in establishing the
Methodist Book Concern on the basis on which it has
since stood, and subsequently, in discharging the still
more responsible and absorbing duties of the episcopate ;
especially when it is farther considered that it would
take some time to satisfy him, that arguments, which ap-
peared to him so untenable, could ever have possessed
the influence which they seem to have exerted on some
minds

This may suffice in regard to the circumstances
under which the essay was written.   It may be expected
that some explanation will also be given of the delay of
its publication   To some, however, and certainly to the
editor himself, a more interesting inquiry may be, why,
since it is acknowledged to be imperfect, it is published
at all   Immediately after the author's decease the
manuscript was examined, and being found incomplete
was laid aside, not to meet the rude gaze of those who
can pardon no imperfection however unavoidable, but as
a memorial of the last efforts of one, every relic of whom
was precious   Some time after, however, several intimate friends of the deceased, of high standing in the
church, desired to read the manuscript, and after pe-

rusing it strongly urged its publication, as being sufficiently complete to subserve the interests of the church
If, therefore, the reputation of his father, or the cause
of the church, should suffer by the publication of an
unfinished essay, the editor's apology must be, that his
own inclination has yielded to the requests of those
who, both by their official station and superior judgment, had a claim upon his deference.

The principal object of the editor in discharging the
duty thus imposed upon him, has been to follow the original, without any additions or alterations other than
those which were necessary, and which are marked as
such This scrupulous accuracy has occasionally led
to repetition, which by no means characterized the author's usual style The careful reader, however, will
observe that this occurs principally in the quotations;
and will find a sufficient explanation in the fact, that
these quotations were not written out in the manuscript,
but only referred to, so that the repetitions would not
appear until the work was prepared for the press.

As to the subject matter itself of the essay, it will,
perhaps, become the editor to say but little There are
two thoughts, however, which he would desire the
reader to bear in mind while reading this or any similar
tract The first is, that no argument is of any avail in
the controversy with the Methodist Episcopal Church, unless it prove not merely that episcopacy is a proper form
of church government, (for this she herself asserts, and
adopts it as her own,) but also, that no other form of
government is admissible ; nay, more, no other form of
episcopacy than that which is founded upon a distinct
order of bishops, deriving their authority through an uninterrupted succession from the apostles.

The second thought is, that the manner in which
efforts are now made to establish the high-church claims
on the foundation of Scripture, is calculated to lead to

great evil Not that we object to the attempt to test
the question by Scripture, (for undoubtedly this is the
only criterion that should be admitted by Protestant
Christians, and we only regret that high-churchmen
have not submitted to it before,) but to the mode of
carrying it out, by making incidental hints and obscure
intimations the basis of what are alleged to be important doctrines This course, (which has been adopted
in regard to many other dogmas, and with a zeal pro-
portioned to the deficiency of evidence for them,) whatever success it may promise at first, cannot fail to be
ultimately pernicious to religion in general, and of
course to the particular party which pursues it And it
might be well for ultraists of every denomination to
consider what would be gained by securing the sanction of Scripture, if, in the very attempt, we impair the
authority of Scripture itself , like shipwrecked mariners,
who, by their imprudent eagerness sink the long boat on
which they fondly relied for escape In conclusion, the
editor regrets the necessity of taking any part in those
controversies by which the Christian church is dis-
tracted and her strength divided, at a time when all her
forces ought to be combined against the armies of the
alien But it must be remembered that in this dispute
the Methodist Episcopal Church stands on the defen-
sive She interferes not with the claims of other denominations to be regarded as members of the spiritual
body of Christ, but she dare not surrender her own.
She, with others, now stands where the early gentile
Christians stood in opposing the Jewish bigotry of the
temple, and where the ancestors of the present Protestant high-churchmen stood in resisting the usurpations of
papal Rome ; nor will she abandon this post of honour
until exclusionists of every class have surrendered
their peculiar claims to the covenant mercies of God.
  Dickinson College, May 25, 1838.   R E.

EPISCOPACY

THE field over which the episcopal controversy has been spread is one so wide, and marked by the tracks of those who have traversed it in so many various and even cross directions, that he who would thread its mazes without danger of missing the narrow path of truth will require, to use a phrase of Dr Jortin's, more than Ariadne's clew. This consideration of itself, not to mention others which might be named, would deter me from my present undertaking, (which I most sincerely wish were in the hands of those who have both more leisure and ability for the task,) were it not that the continued, or, more properly, the recently renewed attacks, both public and private, of those who set up a claim of divine right to monopolize all ecclesiastical authority, and even the covenant mercies of our Saviour himself, oblige us to expose the futility and the arrogance of their pretensions, and to vindicate the grounds on which, having received help from God, we continue to claim a place, be it even the humblest, among the lawful churches of Christ In the prosecution of this design, earnestly imploring, both for myself and the reader, the guidance of a safer clew than Ariadne's—that wisdom from above which is promised to all that lack and ask—I purpose to divide the following tract into two parts

In the first, I shall consider the subject of episcopacy generally, and in the second, that of the Methodist Episcopal Church in particular *

* [The reader will perceive that this second part of the author's design was never accomplished, and the first has been left incomplete. The author's views, however, of Methodist episcopacy may be in some degree gathered from his ' Defence of our Fathers '—ED]

OF EPISCOPACY IN GENERAL.

Claiming, as the Methodist Episcopal Church does, to be not only a lawful church of Christ, but a lawful *episcopal* church, it is plain that our controversy is not with episcopacy itself, as a form of church polity Our opponents, indeed, evince a great inclination to the begging of this question, and too many among ourselves inconsistently, though inadvertently, strengthen them in the sophism, by conceding to them, both in conversation and in writing, the exclusive title of Episcopalians This ought to be corrected, and the various churches of Christendom distinguished by their proper titles At least each should not be forgetful of *its own* proper designation, nor yield the undue influence of even the exclusive name to those who would and do make unmerited advantage of it: for, as has been well remarked, though names are but sounds, yet those who are conversant in the history of mankind will readily allow that they have greater influence on the opinions of the generality of men than most people are aware of [x] The episcopal form of church polity is ours also. We admit and adopt episcopacy. We admit its agreeableness to the constitution of the Christian church in the apostolical age But still the question remains, *What is episcopacy?* Not what is it that Papists and other high-church exclusionists are

---

*[The reader will be pleased to see, in this connection, the opinion of Coleridge on this subject, as expressed in note 56 of the "Aids to Reflection," where he is objecting to the ordinary application of the words *Unitarian* and *Catholic* .—

"Convinced, as I am, that current appellations are never wholly indifferent or inert, and that, when employed to express the characteristic belief or object of a *religious* confederacy, they exert on the many a great and constant, though insensible, influence,—I cannot but fear that in adopting the former ['the name which the party itself has taken up'] I may be sacrificing the interests of truth beyond what the duties of courtesy can demand or justify "—Ed]

pleased to denominate thus at this day,—but what is
episcopacy in the New Testament sense of the *term* or
of the *thing?* To the pure and sufficient light of the
Holy Scriptures on this subject, our high-church opponents generally seem to think it necessary to add that
also of the writings of the Christian fathers, as they are
styled. Without resorting to this source, indeed, it is
absolutely impossible for them—even those few of them
who profess to confine the argument to the ground of
Scripture—to complete their chain. Without this an
essential link is wanting, as I shall hereafter take occasion to show in regard to a modern writer of this class.
But, although we deny that there is any necessity for
this resort, in any inquiry regarding any point of essential Christian doctrine, morals, ordinances, or church
polity,—believing as we do, and as all *Protestants* ought
to do, in the perfection and entire sufficiency of Scripture alone on every such question,—yet I shall not
object to follow some of them even into this branch of
the inquiry,—satisfied as I am that *their* cause can gain
no just support from this collateral branch of evidence,—
so long as it shall be confined to the Christian writings
of the age immediately succeeding that of the apostles,
and of which neither the genuineness nor the integrity
can be fairly questioned. By the aid of these lights,
my object is to review the grounds which have been
taken in regard to the *essential* constitution of a lawful
episcopal church of Christ. And if, where so much may
be said, and has been said, by learned, wise, and good
men, on opposite sides, there be a strong presumption
of probability, as in most similar cases, that truth lies in
the middle and not in either extreme, I trust to be able
to show that it is precisely this ground—a ground both
liberal and safe—that is occupied by the Methodist
Episcopal Church.

The writers on the high-church side, in general, make
up their issue between diocesan episcopacy, in their

sense of it, as an intrinsically and essentially distinct and superior third order by divine appointment, without which there can be no true Christian church nor valid Christian ministry or ordinances, and parity—that is to say, the presbyterian doctrine, strictly, of but one order of Christian ministers. Let it be distinctly understood, however, that this is not the issue between them and *us* We do indeed admit the validity of presbyterian ordination, but not the presbyterian doctrine of parity We cannot feel at liberty to go so far toward this as even the present assistant bishop of the Protestant Episcopal Church in the commonwealth of Pennsylvania, Dr. *II U. Onderdonk* * We dare not say with him, "If we cannot authenticate the claims of the episcopal office, we will surrender those of our deacons, and let all power be confined to the one office of presbyters."† By no means The Scriptural evidence for the order of deacons, as an order of ministers distinct from that of presbyters or bishops, is too plain to be thus lightly treated. The directions of St. Paul to Timothy, (1 Tim iii, 8–13,) not to mention other passages, are too explicit and solemn to allow *us* to surrender this order *in any event* Let it stand on its own ground, whether we can authenticate that of bishops or not; "for they that have used the office of a deacon well, purchase to themselves a good degree," to which their title ought not to be made dependent on the claims of others to any other degree

I ought, indeed, to do the last-quoted author the justice to say, and I do it with pleasure, that he subscribes not to the extreme opinion that episcopacy is essential to the being of a church ‡ I wish that what he says in some other parts of the tract cited could fairly be reconciled with this candid and commendable concession, which

---

* [The reader will recollect that this was written before the death of the then bishop of Pennsylvania, Dr White —Ed]

† Episcopacy Tested by Scripture, p. 11   ‡ Ibid , p. 5.

his sense of truth, after all his investigations, compelled
him to make   In one respect he seems to go far beyond
even the venerable senior bishop of the Protestant
Episcopal Church, whose assistant he is   Dr. White,*
with that leading champion of high church, Hooker,
distinctly admitted the plea of "the exigence of necessity," for departing from the fancied apostolical succession in the high-church sense; and I have not understood that this admission has ever been retracted,
although the pamphlet containing it, which was originally published in 1783 was republished in the city of
his own residence, under the auspices of some of his
own episcopal charge, within a few years past, and
although the authority of his opinion, as an *argumentum
ad hominem*, has been repeatedly referred to in this controversy   His assistant, Dr O , on the contrary, seems
to think that his (Dr O 's) essay settles the point that
episcopacy, in his sense of it, is a "divine appointment," and then affirms that, from such an appointment,
"*no* plea can be strong enough to release us † The
word "no" he himself makes emphatic, as is here done
Indeed, on this ground, and in the same note, p 40, he
seems to suppose—where the sacraments cannot be obtained through such an apostolic ministry, that is to
say, through the high-church succession contended for—
it would be better to dispense with them altogether, as
being "not absolutely, but only generally, necessary to
salvation   Does this writer then really think that there
is just as plain *Scriptural* evidence, (for to this single
ground of argument he sets out with professing strictly
to confine his essay,) of an unbroken series of high-
church bishops from the apostles down to himself, by
divine appointment,—not excepting Alex. VI , of Rome,
and other similar links of the chain,—and that conformity to this pattern is of universal and perpetual obliga-

* Case of the Episcopal Churches in the United States Considered.
† Episcopacy Tested by Scripture, p 40

tion, as that the sacraments of baptism and the Lord's supper are of divine institution and thus binding? It may be answered, perhaps, that the very supposition of "Scriptural" evidence of such a thing involves an utter and palpable absurdity I grant it But who is it that gives occasion for the absurdity? Does not the writer alluded to place the obligation of conforming to a ministry claiming exclusive title through that alleged succession, on a ground not merely equal, but even superior to that which binds us to the observance of the sacraments themselves? And yet he himself concedes, in the commencement of his essay, that no argument is worth taking into the account that has not a palpable bearing on the *Scriptural evidence* of episcopacy;—nay, that episcopacy itself (and certainly then the prelatical succession) is not essential to the being of a church The high-church succession against the sacraments! And Dr. Onderdonk, a Protestant, thinks, if we cannot have both, that we ought rather to give up the latter! Is that succession then "absolutely" necessary to salvation or only "generally" so, on his own principles? Is the evidence that diocesan bishops, in the high-church sense, should uninterruptedly succeed to the office and powers of the apostles, and the observance of this order in the churches be imperatively binding, by divine appointment, through all time, as plain *from Scripture*, (the only ground of argument on the question "worth taking into account,") as that the sacraments are of divine institution and thus imperatively binding?* I am not arguing with Quakers, but with Protestant Episcopalians. What answer do *they* give? Until it can be answered in the affirmative, an essential link in Dr O 's wire-drawn chain is clearly wanting. Could it even be supplied, which it never can, still the claims of the pre-

---

* [This sentence is stricken out in the original, but as its place has not been supplied, and as something of the kind is necessary to the construction of the succeeding sentences, it is here restored.—Ed]

latical succession and of the sacraments would only stand on *equal* ground. As it is, we admire that any *Protestant*, at least, can for a moment hesitate between them *

How much more "apostolical" and rational are the sentiments of Dr. White, now the senior bishop in the same church and in the same diocese. Indeed, as he assumes, "even those who hold episcopacy to be of divine right conceive the obligation to it to be not binding when that idea would be destructive of public worship." "Much more," he justly continues, "must *they* think so who indeed venerate and prefer that form as the most ancient and eligible, but without any idea of divine right in the case. This," he adds, "the author [Dr. White] believes to be the sentiment of the great body of Episcopalians in America, in which respect they have in their favour,

---

* That the reader may have an opportunity to judge whether I have in any manner misunderstood Dr O. on this important point, I subjoin the whole passage, remarking only, in addition, that by "the apostolical or Scriptural ministry," I of course understood him to mean that of the uninterrupted high church succession for which he contends, and which *he* allows " to be *divine.*" His language is,—

" It is due to our discussion to add a few remarks on the question whether *necessity* will justify a departure from the apostolical or Scriptural ministry, or the instituting of a new ministry where that cannot be obtained? On this subject the first point to be determined is, what *is* ' necessity' ? ' Absolute necessity,' to assume the functions of the ministry, never can exist, salvation is not indissolubly connected with the offices of a pastor; the sacraments are not absolutely, but only ' generally necessary to salvation,'—those who cannot obtain them not being required to partake of them. Difficulties long insuperable, preventing the attainment of an important object, form the next species of ' necessity,' and that which is usually referred to in this argument. And here several questions arise. Are the difficulties *insuperable*? Have they been *long* insuperable? Is the object so *important* as to justify deviation from an institution allowed to be *divine*? There should be no reasonable doubt on either of these points.

" In our opinion the last of the above questions can never be justly answered in the affirmative, *no* plea can be strong enough to release us from *divine* appointments. What God has instituted for his church he will preserve in his church, and diffuse through it, till the institution be abrogated by him or is about to be so. This appears to us so clear a dictate of faith, so fundamental a religious truth, that we will not argue for it, it is an axiom, or, at least, an undeniable postulate, and it ought to settle the whole matter." Page 40, note E. [The words in italics are printed as in the original.—Ed.]

unquestionably, the sense of the Church of England, and, as he believes, the opinions of her most distinguished prelates for piety, virtue, and abilities "* Again:—To make any particular form of church government, though adopted by the apostles, unalterably binding, Dr. White maintains, "it must be shown enjoined in positive precept"† He remarks farther that Dr Calamy having considered it as the sense of the church [of England], "in the preface to the ordinal, that the three orders were of divine appointment, and urged it as a reason for nonconformity,—the bishop, [Hoadly,] *with evident propriety*, remarks that the service pronounces *no such thing,* and that, therefore, Dr Calamy created a difficulty where the church had made none—there being 'some difference,' says he, 'between these two sentences —Bishops priests, and deacons are three distinct orders in the church *by divine appointment,*—and, *From the apostles' time* there have been, in Christ's church, bishops, priests, and deacons" "The same distinction," says Dr White, "is *actually drawn and fully proved* by Stillingfleet in the Irenicum"

"Now," continues Dr White, "if the form of church government rest on no other foundation than ancient and apostolical *practice,* it is humbly submitted to consideration whether Episcopalians will not be thought *scarcely deserving the name of Christians* should they, rather than consent to a temporary deviation, abandon every ordinance of positive and divine appointment "‡

Now I suppose that Dr W. and the "distinguished prelate" to whom he refers, to go no farther, had probably examined both the Scriptures and the fathers with as much care and capacity as Dr O , or even as *Dr Cooke,*—a medical gentleman devoted to a different profession,—who, "after six weeks' close inquiry," as he informs us, jumps to such " a thorough conviction" as

---

* Case of the Episcopal Church in the United States Considered, p. 25.
   † Ibid   ‡ Ibid , p 22 and note

leads him to undertake to enlighten the world with a book of such episcopal ultraism as would not discredit Rome itself,—such a one as not even the ablest prelates of the Church of England, in the judgment of Dr. White, himself concurring, with all the predisposing and surrounding circumstances to bias them to that side, and after more than *six years* of "close inquiry," would have had the temerity to usher into the world True learning, sanctified by piety, is always modest And if there be any question debated among Christians on which their moderation ought to appear to all men, this is one,—a question, not concerning the vital and fundamental doctrines of our holy religion, nor even the essential being of a Christian church,—but merely concerning its form of polity, as different branches of the church, in different times and in different places and circumstances, may conceive the same to be most consonant to the principles and objects of Christianity, and best calculated to promote vital and practical godliness in the earth

But I beg pardon This is not Dr. C.'s ground His system admits of no such moderation. Although a very recent convert to it, at the time of undertaking his book, he goes far beyond Dr. Onderdonk, Dr. White, and the most distinguished, pious, virtuous, and able prelates of the mother Church of England itself. With him it is a question of life or death, neck or nothing, church or no church. Indeed, the language which, over and over, he quotes with approbation, as "most unexceptionable," seems to my poor apprehension, to be little, if any, short of absolute blasphemy. It is almost too revolting to be repeated. Of this I shall afford the reader an opportunity to judge in the sequel ; remarking here, by the way, that this gentleman might as hopefully undertake to persuade this generation to adopt the sentiments of the famous "Apostolical Constitutions," which, as the learned Archdeacon Jortin remarks, "repeat it over

and over, lest Christians should chance to forget it—
that a bishop is a god, a god upon earth, and a king,
and infinitely superior to a king, and ruling over rulers
and kings" "Here is strange language indeed! even
far beyond all *eminencies* and *holinesses*"* In the judgment of an eminent critic,† the sentiments contained in
the "Apostolical Constitutions" bear a very near resem-
blance to those in the epistles attributed to Ignatius and
cited by Dr. Cooke. According to these, indeed, the
reverence due to CHRIST himself is less than that which
is due to the *bishop* That which we owe to Christ is
made the measure of the reverence due to "the deacons,"—the lowest order; while "the *bishop*" is to be
reverenced "as the Father,"—evidently meaning GOD
"the Father,"—in whose place he is alleged to preside
in the church Could any language more clearly betray
the hand of the forger of some later age? Will any
friend of the holy and humble Ignatius—the disciple of
John, whose epistles are the very model of simplicity,—
will any such believe that that plain and pious man, on
the very eve of martyrdom, and *himself a bishop*, would
have used such language, and urged and illustrated it
again and again, that we might be sure not to mistake
or forget it? It is incredible; or, if credible, it stamps
the name of Ignatius with a stigma from which we
would fain rescue it Before Dr C's pattern of episcopacy can be embraced, (for what he quotes as "most
unexceptionable," will be taken as his own,) we must
believe that St Paul made a great mistake when he
drew the picture of the man of sin sitting in the temple
of God as God, for this, we have now to learn, is the
very character of a true Christian bishop, though not
such a one as Paul describes to Timothy, nor as his son
Timothy himself Why, then, should we any longer be
offended with the style of "our lord god, the pope"? Is

* Remarks on Ecclesiastical History, vol 1, pp. 154, 155.
† Dr. Campbell

it any worse than (*horresco referens*) our lord god, the *bishop?**

Consistently enough with the above, the Ignatius of Dr C. is guilty of the profanity of staking his own soul as, "*security for them that submit to their bishop,* with their presbyters and deacons," (the latter classes of whom, however, be it remembered, being themselves bound to obey their bishop as "the source of all authority,")† averring that "whatsoever he [the bishop] *shall approve of, that is also pleasing unto God;*" and accordingly, in another place, "*that we ought to look upon the bishop even as we would do upon the Lord himself*" Epistles to Polycarp, the Smyrneans, and the Ephesians. Appendix, pp 6, 22, 24

Fine times, truly, for bishops, if these doctrines can be made to prevail, (and a new and certain way to heaven, which neither our Lord nor any of the apostles ever discovered,—*implicit obedience to the bishop;*) especially, if we add one other very remarkable dictum of this Ignatius, as adduced by Dr. C, viz. —"The more any one sees his bishop *silent,* the more let him revere him" Ibid, p 6   That is, it would seem, the

---

* It may be proper to mention, for the information of general readers, that there are two sets of epistles in the name of Ignatius: one denominated the *larger,* and the other the *shorter* or *smaller*   The larger are given up by critics as confessedly interpolated, which demonstrates that some forger did make free with the name of Ignatius.   The smaller, Dr C pronounces "most unexceptionable, and—written in the very spirit of an ardently pious Christian," p 67   Yet, only two pages before, he had quoted Dr. Lardner with applause as saying that, after a careful comparison of the two, he was of opinion that "even the smaller epistles may have been tampered with by the Arians, or the orthodox, or both," p 65   .

He then asserts that the interpolations in these epistles respected the Arian controversy, which had nothing to do with the subject of church government, and immediately afterward adds, " It is evident, therefore, that there is not the slightest ground to suspect the interpolation of passages to favour episcopacy "   I do not at all perceive the force of this logic, and shall hereafter take occasion more fully to expose its futility.   But the eulogy of Dr C warrants at least the inference that he considers whatever these epistles contain on the subject of episcopacy as "most unexceptionable "   This is sufficient for my present purpose.

† Dr. Cooke, p. 19

2

more he resembles the "dumb dogs" denounced by Isaiah, and, consequently, the less he resembles the prophets who were commanded to "cry aloud" and "spare not," lifting up their "voice like a trumpet," or Bishop Timothy, whom Paul charged to "preach the word,—instant in season and out of season," "reproving, rebuking, exhorting;" or Paul himself, who "taught publicly and from house to house,—testifying both to the Jews and also to the Greeks—warning every one, night and day, with tears;"—the less, I say, a bishop, according to Dr C.'s favourite Ignatius, resembles these, the more he ought to be revered. On this singular sentiment, Dr Campbell well remarks·—Consequently, if, like the Nazianzene monk celebrated by Gregory, a bishop should, in praise of God, devote his tongue to an inviolable taciturnity, he would be completely venerable. This, as the same able author adds, one would be tempted to think, originated from some opulent ecclesiastic, who was by far too great a man for preaching; at least, it seems an oblique apology for those who have no objection to any thing implied in a bishopric except the function.*

Now, to perfect the claims of such lords over God's heritage, with their subject presbyters and deacons, nothing more would seem to be wanting but to persuade the Christian world that "WITHOUT THESE THERE IS NO CHURCH." And these are the identical words which Dr. C. triumphantly alleges from Ignatius, and puts in capitals as throwing "a blaze of light on the subject."† They do, indeed,—a burning blaze—quite enough to consume the argument They assert more than Dr. Onderdonk believed—with Dr. C.'s book before him—

---

* Lectures on Ecclesiastical History, p. 102. Nearly akin to this was the injunction to the English bishops in the reign of Edward VI They were enjoined to preach *four times a year*, unless they had a reasonable excuse. Neal's History of the Puritans, vol. i, p. 91.

† Ibid, p. 20. See also p. 19.

or Dr White, the senior bishop of the same church, or the great body of the most distinguished bishops, or others, among *Protestant* Episcopalians, in Europe or America * Yet to such a sweeping conclusion Dr. C. suddenly leaps over the heads of all these, assuring us, at the same time, that *he* had always been in the habit of requiring strong evidence upon any subject, and never yielding assent to any thing that was not supported by it This, then, I suppose, may be regarded as a specimen of his incredulity without strong evidence, although eminent and candid critics have been compelled to admit that much of what has been imposed upon the world in the name of the meek and holy Ignatius is demonstrably spurious, and that, in consequence, so great a degree of uncertainty has been thrown even upon the rest as to render it extremely difficult even for those most deeply versed in ecclesiastical antiquities and literary criticism, after many years of close investigation, to distinguish what is genuine and true from what is interpolated and false. Let it be distinctly understood that what is above said, or may hereafter be said, for I shall resume this point in another place, is by no means intended to detract in the least from the just merits of that aged and venerable martyr, whose name and memory are entitled to the highest respect; but, for this very reason, to save him, if possible, as Dr Campbell observes, "from a second martyrdom in his works, through the attempts not of open enemies, but of deceitful [I would rather say, of credulous, or injudicious] friends "†

Unlimited and implicit subjection then, as has been shown, on the part of the whole people, not only to the bishop, but to the whole clerical order, is the doctrine of Ignatius as quoted and underwritten by Dr. C.,—

---

* [At this part of the manuscript there are memoranda indicating that the author intended to say more upon the subject —Ed]

† Lectures, p 103

urged too, as it is, by the supreme motive of thereby infallibly securing their salvation, on the pledge of his own soul for it.

In the progress of that species of absolute episcopal lordship, *by divine right*, for which Dr C pleads, he undertakes to show, p 99, that terms, corresponding with the model of those alleged from Ignatius, were used in Tertullian's time also, conveying the very idea that a bishop ruled as "a king" and "master" At p 47, he quotes from Hilary too, with apparent approbation, after Dr Bowden, that "the bishop is the *vicegerent of Christ, and represents his person*"* The legitimate and natural fruit of such doctrines began to exhibit itself, and laid the true foundation of the papacy, so early as in the days of Jerome, in the fourth century. This may be seen in a passage quoted from Jerome by Dr. C. himself, though for a very different purpose. Of some of the bishops even of that time, Jerome testifies that, "as if placed upon some lofty eminence, they scarce deign to see mortals and to speak to their fellow-servants," p. 113 Lofty, indeed! And if the sentiments cited by Dr C. as "most unexceptionable," can be triumphantly established, and on the basis of *divine right*, similar fruit, in process of time, (such is poor human nature,) must and will again appear. And how far civil liberty itself could long be safe under such a system of absolute spiritual despotism, bound upon the neck of the prostrate people by the supreme sanction of divine appointment, the history of the past must instruct us, or we must remain uninstructed, or learn from sad experiment

I am truly glad, however, for the sake of our common Christianity, and especially for the sake of the

---

* One of these vicegerents and representatives of Christ, in the lineal succession, Bishop Bonner, of England, was in the habit of *beating* his clergy *corporally* when he was displeased with any thing See Bishop Burnet's Abridgment of the History of the Reformation, p 262

clerical order, and, above all, of the episcopal, that Dr. C is not a clergyman. In my poor opinion, a work could scarcely be devised calculated more seriously and justly to prejudice the whole clerical, and especially the episcopal cause,—and through that the cause of Christianity,—although I am far from believing that Dr. C. intended this. It has been his zeal in the service of a newly adopted communion that has probably led him to overshoot his mark. And the chief wonder is that any clergyman, and, above all, any bishop, unless indeed it were he of Rome, should eulogize or recommend such a work,—or how any Christian *people*, with *the New Testament in their hands*, can favour or countenance a book which places them, by the alleged authority of Heaven itself, under the yoke of a spiritual domination thus absolute, unlimited, and degrading.

It is related, among other ancient ecclesiastical legends, of a certain monk whom Satan would have drawn into heresy by asking his opinion on a certain point, that he prudently answered, "*Id credo quod credit ecclesia.*" [I believe what the church believes] But, said Satan, thinking to ensnare him, "*Quid credit ecclesia?*" [What does the church believe?] The wary monk replied, "*Id quod ego credo.*" [What I believe.] And thus, says Jortin,* if Nestorius would have slept in his own bed, he should have said, "*Id credo quod credit sanctissimus Cyrillus.*" [I believe what the most holy Cyril believes] Cyril was bishop of Alexandria in the fifth century. *Implicit faith*, indeed, is the very correlative of *implicit obedience*,—the necessary result of an absolute episcopacy, by divine right, and the genuine seed of all the monstrosities of the papacy itself How different from the doctrine of "the great Paul,"—"Not for that we have dominion over your

---

* Remarks on Ecclesiastical History, vol. i, p. 16.

faith." and of Peter,—"Neither as being lords over God's heritage."

But what makes the matter still worse, if worse can be, as if Dr C were determined to push his scheme of episcopal sovereignty to the utmost possible extreme of autocratical absolutism, he not only exhibits bishops as holding, by divine title, such actual lordship over. God's heritage generally, but over the presbyters in particular, of whom the bishop is "judge and punisher," and against whom, however "partially" he may act,—in other words, tyrannize and sin,—"*there is no redress.*" The inspired Paul himself, had Timothy acted thus after he was constituted a bishop, it would seem according to Dr C, would have had no authority to correct him. or to redress the presbyters; and the appeal even of Paul must have been "to God" alone Such are bishops after Dr. C's pattern; and consequently, I suppose, were Paul himself or the whole college of apostles still on earth, with all their plenary powers, they would be incompetent to afford a particle of redress to any poor presbyter, deacon, or laic, against the partiality or tyranny of any bishop in this succession, though he were an Alexander VI.,—a very Nero among the popes themselves,—for, against such "there is no redress."*

* If it seem incredible to the reader that any man, in the 19th century, can think of imposing such a scheme of episcopacy upon *Protestant* Christians, I refer him to the whole passage in Dr C's book, p 8,—remembering that it is to be taken in connection with his theory of Timothy's episcopate at Ephesus by the ordination of Paul, and the "most unexceptionable" powers of a bishop elsewhere alleged by him, as above shown What a system is here ! Even the most strenuous advocates of the high church nonjuring bishops of England who maintained the indefeasible, hereditary, divine right of kings, and the absolute unlawfulness of resistance on the part of the people, under any provocation or pretext whatever, yet admitted that a bishop might be deposed by an ecclesiastical council Many Papists, too, admit this in regard even to the pope But, if Bishop Timothy "act partially," and, of course, sin, in this or in any other way, for the principle is the same, what is the remedy ? An appeal to Paul ? Nay his "apostolical rod" must not touch the *bishop* What then ? An appeal to the whole college of apostles in council ? Equally vain The "rod" of the whole of them is unequal to this exigence. "There is no redress, and the appeal of Paul

A favourite position of the advocates of episcopal ultraism is, that the divine Founder of the Christian ministry intended, in its original institution, to conform it to the model of the Jewish priesthood and temple service According to this theory it is alleged that the episcopate succeeds to the rank and prerogatives of the high-priesthood, while the presbyters take the place of the priests, and the deacons of the Levites The groundlessness of this alleged parallel has been often exposed, and yet there are not wanting writers who continue to repeat it Mosheim, indeed, charitably admits, as "highly probable, that they who first introduced this absurd comparison of offices so entirely distinct, did it rather through ignorance and error than through artifice and design ;" though, as he remarks, the notion when once introduced, being industriously propagated, produced its natural pernicious effects, and was made a new source both of honour and profit to the doctors who had the good fortune to persuade the people into the belief of it

If the Christian church was constituted on the plan of any Jewish model, there is much stronger evidence that it was that of the synagogue than that of the temple. This has been, as many think, very successfully demonstrated by Stillingfleet and others I shall not, however, trouble the reader with a detail of the arguments which sustain this position, but shall content

---

is to God " So says Dr C , and, be it remembered, according to him, the episcopate of Timothy, by divine right, is the one only essential model of a valid Christian episcopacy—without which there can be no true church, ministry, or ordinances—throughout the world, and until the appearing of our Lord Jesus Christ

But, were it even admitted that an oppressed presbyter might appeal to an ecclesiastical council, how, according to Dr C , would it be necessary that it should be composed ?

[A portion of what is here given in the form of a note seems to have been intended to take the place of a part of the text, but, as the necessary alterations were not made in the manuscript by the author, the whole is here inserted, though liable, in some degree, to the charge of repetition —ED]

myself with the single observation that, if the parallel
be a correct one,—one founded in divine appointment
as the allegation is,—then it is a most unfortunate one
for *Protestant* Episcopalians; for, most unquestionably,
in the alleged model there was but *one* high priest, and
could be but one, legitimately, at a time. Consequently
the pattern is violated in its most important and essential features,—in its very head,—if there be more than
one bishop at a time over the whole Christian church,
as there was but one high priest at a time over the
whole Jewish church At any rate, nothing short of one
supreme, universal bishop can at all satisfy the parallel.
Now this argument would be very appropriate, and entitled to the merit of consistency at least, in the mouth
of the pope or of his partizans But how it can serve
the cause of *Protestant* Episcopalians, who maintain
not only an unlimited plurality but the perfect official
equality of all bishops throughout the world, is more
than I have wit to penetrate. How the hereditariness
of the Jewish high-priesthood is legitimately reconciled,
in the parallel, with the celibacy of the Romish priesthood, I have not understood A Protestant pope,
should one ever be set up, might more consistently put
in a claim for this feature in it

Again, however, I am reminded that Dr. C stops not
at the pattern even of the high-priesthood of Aaron.
The supreme, controlling power of "Moses," with the
subordinate rule of the seventy elders, he thinks "a
form of government as much like the episcopal as one
thing can be like another," p. 116 If he means the
papal episcopal, some analogy must be granted, so far
at least as to the "form" of one and one only supreme
earthly chief over the whole people. But if the *protestant* episcopal be meant, then even the trace of
analogy must be denied; and I should suppose all
Protestants, Dr C, I am sorry to say, excepted, would
join in the denial.

Indeed Dr C seems not satisfied that even Moses' government was that of the archetype in the divine will and preference   Have we then not yet reached his ultimatum of individual absolutism?   It seems not   In his opinion that part of the model which consisted in the appointment of *elders* to assist Moses "was not the plan God instituted for Moses "   This he expressly asserts ; and then, that there may be no mistake about it, immediately adds in the succeeding sentence, ' He [God] set him [Moses] over the people alone," p 117. The meaning, doubtless, is,—Set him alone over the people   He seems even dissatisfied with the meek and diffident Moses for beseeching "God to give him help to rule over the people ;" and adds that, although the request was granted, it was, nevertheless, with "marked displeasure" on the part of the Almighty   The whole paragraph, in connection with the preceding, demonstrates, to the best of my understanding, that Dr C. would have thought it better if Moses had continued to rule the people "alone" without the help of elders   And if so in the Jewish type, as alleged, why not in the Christian antitype?   If his holiness, the sovereign pontiff, ever saw or shall yet see this argument, it might well bring from him an offering of gratitude to the author, but how it can from any *protestant* bishop, elder, deacon, or laic, I must again profess myself utterly at a loss to imagine   Scarcely less gratitude, one would think, is due from Rome for the very strong testimony alleged out of Irenæus, by Dr C, in behalf of that "greatest, most ancient, and universally known church, founded and constituted at Rome by the two most glorious apostles, Peter and Paul "—" *For with this church*," [Dr C himself marks it emphatically, as is here done,] *on account of its greater pre-eminence, it is necessary that every church should agree ;* that is, *those which are in all respects faithful*," pp 71, 72   If the argument be a good one in the *episcopal* controversy, why not in every other? Thank you, protestant Dr., might Rome well say.

I have heard of a Protestant Episcopal clergyman, not one thousand miles from where I write, who, in labouring to seduce one of our ministers from his fidelity to his own church, I regret to say it, by the mercenary temptation, among other means, of a vacant parish, (a species of conduct in which there is too much reason to believe he has not been singular,) alleged in argument that the Protestant Episcopal Church in this country is the chief barrier to the progress of the Papists, and ours a hinderance to the successful resistance of this barrier And this gentleman, I believe, was also an admirer and recommender of Dr C.'s book. With the Protestant Episcopal Church and its clergy generally, we neither seek nor desire controversy. We should be most happy to agree with them, especially in withstanding sin and Satan in every form. But if the extravagant pretensions of Rome are ever to be successfully resisted, surely we may say of the work before us,—

"Non talibus armis, nec defensoribus istis."

After drawing such a picture of episcopacy, and attempting to establish it on such a basis, Dr C remarks, —"Of this state of things in the church, evidence more and more abounds as we *progress* through the third century For this he assigns the following curious reasons :—"Because," as he continues, "more and more learning was enlisted in the cause of the Christian religion, and because more of the writings of the fathers of the succeeding centuries have been preserved" It seems not to have occurred to him, or at least not to have been judged expedient to be mentioned to his readers, that it was rather "because" of the increasing corruptions and usurpations that ensued, through which the whole face of the church was changed, and the bishops of the succeeding ages, leaving the simplicity of their predecessors, were elevated to the rank, the titles, the immunities, and the powers of sovereign lords. To deny this fact, one must either be ignorant of all history or shut his eyes against its clearest light

The seeds of this state of things were sown, I grant, though probably without even dreaming of their ultimate fruit, at a comparatively early period   Even *Cyprian*, the famous bishop of Carthage in the middle of the third century, whose writings are as confidently cited by some eminent men *against* the exclusive claims of diocesan episcopacy by divine institution, as by others *for* them, seems, undesignedly, to have at times used language in the florid style of his country and age, which Papists allege as containing the very essential principles of the popedom   I say undesignedly,—because Cyprian himself showed this in his own noble resistance of the imperious Stephen of Rome.   One of the famous sayings of Cyprian, as alleged in the no less famous Council of Trent, was, that throughout the whole Christian church "there is *but one bishopricke*, and every bishop holdeth a part thereof *in solidum* "*

This ingenious and fruitful idea was more largely developed and amplified in the same council by Father Laynez, general of the Jesuits   That saying of Cy-

---

* Historie of the Councell of Trent, by Fra Paolo Sarpi, p 599   There is a singular expression seeming to look this way, though obscurely, in one of the epistles of Cornelius, bishop of Rome, to Fabius, bishop of Antioch He is speaking of his rival, Novatus, as Eusebius names him, (or Novatian, according to Mosheim.) whom he berates most roundly, and, among other things, remarks as follows —" Wherefore this jolly defender of the gospell was ignorant that there ought to be but one bishop in the catholicke [universal] church " (Eusebius' Ecclesiastical History, lib vi, ch 42   The original Greek of Eusebius, as quoted by Lord King, is, " Ουκ ηπιστατο ἑνα επισκοπον δειν ειναι εν καθολικη εκκλησια "   And his reference is to chap xliii, according to the Greek original)   Why did Cornelius style the Church of Rome the Catholic Church?   Did Cyprian borrow the idea, or did Cornelius take it from Cyprian?   They were contemporaries and correspondents

prian, he argued, "is to bee expounded that the whole power is placed in one pastor, without division, who doth impart and communicate it to his fellow-ministers as cause doth require. And in this sence *Ciprian* maketh the Apostolique *Sea* like unto a roote, an head, a fountaine, and the sunne, shewing, by these comparisons, that jurisdiction is essential in that alone, and in others by derivation or participation. And this is the meaning," he adds, "of the words so much used by antiquity, that *Peter* and the pope have fulnesse of power, and the others are of their charge " As a matter of curiosity, it may perhaps gratify the reader to see a little more of the Jesuit general's amplification of the idea of Cyprian. "And that he [the pope, continues the general] is the onely pastor, is plainely proved by the words of CHRIST, when he said, He hath other sheepe which he will gather together, and so one sheepfold should be made, and one shepheard The shepheard meant in that place cannot be CHRIST, because he would not speake in the future, that there shall be one shepheard, himself then being a shepheard, and therefore it must be understood of another shepheard which was to be constituted after him, which can be no other but *Peter* and his successors " To cap the climax of this argument, the ingenious general, criticising that passage of Christ to Peter, "Feed my sheep," avers that the term "sheep" there signifies "*animals*, which have no part or judgment in governing themselves."* I by no means intend to insinuate, however, that this criticism is concurred in by Dr C , for, although he maintains, as "most unexceptionable," the sentiment alleged from Ignatius of implicit subjection to the bishop, as "in the place of God," yet it is, I presume of course, as men, and not as brute "animals,"—although I must confess, on farther thought, that such a yoke would seem to be

* Historie of the Councell of Trent, by Fra Paolo Sarpi, p. 611.

rather more galling on the necks of rational and Christian men than even on those of brute "animals."*

But as Dr C makes the testimony of Ignatius, identified as he thinks it with that of Polycarp and Irenæus afterward, a main pillar of his castle, I am not yet done with this father. The epistles ascribed to him are the first of the ecclesiastical writing of antiquity which mentioned bishops, presbyters, and deacons, as three distinct orders in the Christian church He is supposed by some to have written about the sixteenth year of the second century, and by some even earlier. Dr. C. quotes the opinion of Dr Lardner, as before stated, that his smaller epistles as well as the larger may have been tampered with by the Arians or the orthodox, or both; and from this, after a little preparation of the reader, in regard to the Arian controversy, he skips to the conclusion,—"It is evident, therefore, that there is not the slightest ground to suspect the interpolation of passages to favour episcopacy." Now, to me, this is strange logic How the admission that they may have been tampered with in one important respect makes it "evident" that there is not the slightest ground to suspect that they have been tampered with in any other, I cannot perceive Let the argument be put into form, and it runs thus.—

The larger epistles of Ignatius are certainly spurious; and even the smaller may have been tampered with by the Arians or the orthodox, or both.

Therefore, it is evident that there is not the slightest ground to suspect that they were ever interpolated on the subject of episcopacy.

---

* After Christianity became the established and ruling religion, tumults, seditions, and even massacres, sometimes took place at the elections of bishops This was the natural result of such doctrines of episcopal dignity and supremacy See Jortin's Remarks on Ecclesiastical History, vol. i, p. 414.

And yet this is very much the manner in which **Dr. C** draws conclusions and makes assertions in various places of his book

The interpolations of the epistles of Ignatius being admitted by eminent and candid critics of all parties, it cannot be safe to found any decision in this controversy on the testimony of an author with whose works transcribers have confessedly made so free   If they were interpolated with regard to important doctrines, why may they not have been also in regard to church polity? Did not the indisputable progress of clerical usurpation, and especially of episcopal domination and arrogance, in the following ages, afford at least an equal temptation to such *pious frauds?*   The "*Apostolical Constitutions*" is also a work of antiquity, pretended to have been written even by the twelve apostles and St. Paul together with Clemens for their *amanuensis.*   It is a work, too, the sentiments of which on episcopacy, as I have before shown in a quotation from Dr Jortin, are obviously similar to those ascribed to Ignatius ; and it is not a little remarkable, in this connection, that such critics as Le Clerc and the "learned and ingenious" Bruno, as Dr Jortin testifies, had a suspicion that an *Arian* bishop of the fourth century, Leontius, was the inventor or the interpolator of these Constitutions also.*   For, be it remembered that, not long after their rise in the fourth century, the Arians not only had their bishops, but, through the favour of Constantine in his latter days, and especially of his son Constantius, became the dominant sect.   And how likely the Arian as well as the orthodox bishops of that and some following ages may have been to perpetrate such impositions on the ignorant may be conjectured from the state assumed by this said Arian prelate, Leontius.   It is cer-

---

* Dr Campbell thinks they were a compilation probably begun in the third century, and ended in the fourth or fifth   Lectures, p 99

tain, says Jortin, that he carried his head high enough;
and sent word to the empress Eusebia, who is said to
have been haughty, that he would not comply with her
request and pay her a visit, unless she would promise
to bow down before him and receive his blessing, and
then to stand up while he sat, until he should give her
leave to sit down, which put the lady into a violent
rage.*

Now even the Apostolical Constitutions might be of
service on several accounts, as they contain many
things undoubtedly true, in regard both to the doctrines and the discipline of the ancient church; but the
whole are so blended with insertions of a later date that
it is now beyond human skill, as the last-named eminent
critic remarks, to make the separation with any certainty.
And, should their authority appear only ambiguous, as
he had before observed, it would be our duty to reject
them, lest we should adopt, as divine doctrines, the commandments of men   This is precisely our view of the
epistles ascribed to Ignatius   That he did write epistles,
shortly before his martyrdom. is not in the least doubted.
Neither is it disputed that what he wrote, especially in
regard to facts within his own knowledge, or to the
traditions received from the apostles or their contemporaries, could we separate with any certainty what is
genuine and authentic from what is spurious and false,
would be entitled to high regard   *Against* our opponents, indeed, in this controversy, whatever is to our
purpose in the testimony even of Ignatius, a witness of
their own introduction, may well be urged, for though,
as Dr Campbell judiciously remarks, the work ascribed
to him is, with reason, suspected to have been interpolated with a view to aggrandize the episcopal order, it
was never suspected of any interpolation with a view to
lessen it †

* Remarks on Ecclesiastical History, vol i, p 156.
† Dr Jortin, after rejecting altogether the larger epistles ascribed to Igna-

Among the arguments which render suspicious the integrity of the epistles ascribed to Ignatius, as regards church polity, the following are advanced by Dr. Campbell —

"What makes his testimony the more to be suspected is, first, because the forementioned distinction [of three orders] is so frequently and officiously obtruded on the reader, sometimes not in the most modest and becoming terms, as was the manner of the apostles, when speaking of their own authority, and obedience is enjoined to the bishop and presbyters, even where the injunction cannot be deemed either natural or pertinent, as in his epistle to Polycarp, who was himself a bishop Secondly, because the names bishop and presbyter are never used by him for expressing the same office, as they had been uniformly used by all who had preceded him, and were occasionally used by most of the ecclesiastic writers of that century.   Thirdly and principally, because Polycarp, a contemporary and surviver of Ignatius, in a letter to the Philippians, quoted in a former discourse, pointing out the duties of all ranks, pastors and people, makes mention of only two orders of ministers, to wit presbyters and deacons, in the same manner as Luke, and

tius as clearly spurious, adds the observation, that although the shorter are, on many accounts, preferable to the larger, yet he would not affirm that even they had undergone no alteration at all —*Remarks on Ecclesiastical History*, vol 1, p 227.   The same author says that "Origen, and other ancient Christians, ascribe to our Saviour this saying —Τινεσθε δοκιμοι τραπεζιται, ταμεν αποδοκιμαζοντες, το δε καλον κατεχοντες , that is, *act like skilful bankers, rejecting what is bad, and retaining what is good*   This precept,' continues the archdeacon, "is proper for all who apply themselves to the study of religious antiquities.   Good and bad money is offered to them , and they ought to beware of the coin which will not pass current in the republic of letters and in the critical world and of that which is found light when weighed in the balance of the sanctuary " Ibid , pp 420, 421   This advice, whether truly handed down from our Saviour or not, is worthy of a man of letters and a Christian divine ; and the latter part of it especially the plainest reader may follow, and will do well to follow, though he may not have the good fortune to be of the republic of letters, or conversant with the critical world   Let him weigh *in the balance of the sanctuary*, then, the extravagant episcopal ultraism which Dr C so often alleges from the sophisticated Ignatius, as *essential* to *the very being of a church*, and the result is not feared.

Paul, and Clement had done before him, nay, and recommends to the people submission to them, and only to them, in terms which, I must say, were neither proper nor even decent, if these very ministers had a superior in the church to whom they themselves, as well as the people, were subject   To me, the difference between these two writers appears by no means as a diversity in style, but as a repugnancy in sentiment.   They cannot be both made applicable to the same state of the church; so that we are forced to conclude, that in the writings of one or the other there must have been something spurious or interpolated   Now I have heard no argument urged against the authenticity of Polycarp's letter equally cogent as some of the arguments employed against the authenticity of the epistles of Ignatius.   And, indeed, the state of the church, in no subsequent period, can well account for such a forgery as the epistle of the former to the Philippians; whereas the ambition of the ecclesiastics, for which some of the following centuries were remarkable. renders it extremely easy to account for the nauseous repetition of obedience and subjection to the bishop, presbyters, and deacons, to be found in the letters of Ignatius "*

Again —" It is not only what we find singular in them for so early a period, relating to the different orders of ministers in the church, which has raised suspicions of their authenticity, or, at least, of their integrity; there are other causes which have co-operated in producing the same effect · one is, the style, in many places, is not suited to the simplicity of the times immediately succeeding the times of the apostles.   It abounds with inflated epithets, unlike the humble manner of the inspired writers, and in this, as in other respects, seems more formed on that which became fashionable after the acquisition of greater external importance, which

* Lecture on Ecclesiastical History, pp. 96, 7

3

opulence never fails to bring, and after the discussion of certain theological questions agitated in the third and fourth centuries, to which we find, sometimes, a manifest allusion. What I am going to observe has much the appearance of anachronism, which often betrays the hand of the interpolator. The expression, *the church which is in Syria*, occurs twice. Now nothing can be more dissimilar to the dialect which had prevailed in the apostolic age, and which continued to prevail in the second century. Except when *the church* denoted the whole Christian community, it meant no more than a single congregation."* Now there were many churches in Syria in the days of Ignatius, and many bishops. Indeed when, through the increase of converts, a bishop's parish came to contain more people than could be comprehended in one congregation, the custom continued, in contradiction to propriety, of still calling his charge *a church*, in the singular number. But it was not till after the distinction made between the metropolitan and the suffragans, which was about a century later, that this use originated, of calling all the churches of a province the church (not the churches) of such a province. To this they were gradually led by analogy. The metropolitan presided among the provincial bishops, as the bishop among the presbyters. The application of the term was, after the rise of patriarchal jurisdiction, extended still further. All that was under the jurisdiction of the archbishop, or patriarch, was his church.

But it is not the style, only, which has raised suspicion; it is chiefly the sentiments. "Attend to the bishop," says Ignatius to Polycarp, "that God may

* Lord King says that he found the word *church* once used by Cyprian [about the middle of the third century] for a collection of many particular churches, but that, except in this instance, he did not remember ever to have met with it in this sense in any writings, either of Cyprian or the rest of the fathers; but, whenever they would speak of the Christians in any kingdom or province, they always said, in the plural, *the churches;* never in the singular, *the church*, of such a kingdom or province.—Pp 4, 5.

3*

attend to you   I pledge my soul for theirs who are
subject to the bishop, presbyters, and deacons   Let my
part in God be with them." Αντιψυχον εγω των ὑποτασσομενων τω
επισκοπῳ κ. τ λ , which Cotelerius renders *Devovear ego pro
us qui subditi sunt episcopo*, &c.   Admit that, from his
adopting the plural of the imperative προσεχετε, in the
beginning of the paragraph, he is to be considered as
addressing the congregation of Smyrna, and not the
bishop to whom the letter is directed, is there nothing
exceptionable in what he says?   Was it the doctrine of
Ignatius, that all that is necessary to salvation in a
Christian is an implicit subjection to the bishop, presbyters, and deacons?   Be it that he means only in spiritual matters, is this the style of the apostles to their
Christian brethren?   Was it thus that Ignatius exhibited to his followers the pattern which had been given by
that great apostle, who could say of himself and his
fellow apostles, appealing for his voucher to the people's
experience of their ministry, *We preach not ourselves, but
Christ Jesus the Lord, and ourselves your servants, for
Jesus' sake.*"*

On the contrary, as the same author continues a
little after, "is it not his predominant scope, [that of the
assumer of Ignatius' name,] in those letters, to preach
himself and other ecclesiastics, inculcating upon the
people the most submissive, unlimited, and blind obedience to all of the clerical order?   This is an everlast-
ing topic, to which he never slips an opportunity of
recurring, in season and out of season.   The only consistent declaration which would have suited the author
of these epistles, must have been the reverse of Paul's
We preach not Christ Jesus the Lord, but so far only as
may conduce to the increase of our influence, and the
exaltation of our power, nay, for an object so important, we are not ashamed to preach up ourselves your

* Lectures on Ecclesiastical History, pp 100-102.

masters, with unbounded dominion over your faith, and consequently over both soul and body "*

Such, in the judgment of Dr Campbell, are the epistles which Dr. C regards as "most unexceptionable," and which, as before said, constitute a main pillar of his hierarchal edifice.

To strengthen this pillar, moreover, he endeavours to make out that the testimony of Polycarp and Irenæus is identical with that in these epistles

Polycarp was a contemporary and surviver of Ignatius. His writings, in the order of time, were between those of Ignatius and Irenæus, and he suffered martyrdom probably a little before the middle of the second century, or soon after; for chronologists do not exactly agree on this point † Dr C quotes him as saying in his epistle to the Philippians, "The epistles of Ignatius which he wrote unto us, together with what others of his have come to our hands, we have sent to you, according to your order; which are subjoined to this epistle; by which you may be greatly profited,—for they treat of faith, and patience, and of all things that pertain to edification in the Lord Jesus "‡ This, with his strong attestation of Ignatius's personal worth and triumphant end, Dr C says, " show that Polycarp completely agreed with Ignatius in relation to the great concerns of the church   All that we see, therefore, [he continues,] in the passages *in Italics* in the epistles of Ignatius, [that is, what Dr C puts in Italics in these epistles, as printed in his appendix,] stands supported by the evidence of Polycarp, as completely as if he had himself written those epistles."‡

Hold, dear sir.   This is another conclusion too hastily

---

* Lectures on Ecclesiastical History, pp. 100–102.

† There is also considerable diversity among critics as to the exact date of Polycarp's epistle   Dr Jortin says it is supposed to have been written A. D 107, Dr Campbell that it must certainly have been written a considerable time before the middle of the second century.

‡ P 70

sprung to It is a mere *petitio principii*,—a sheer begging of the question It must first be proved that all those passages were in the copy of those epistles which came under the eye of Polycarp; for this, you ought to be aware, is disputed, for reasons already given. Until this difficulty, therefore, is removed, this argument is deficient in an essential link

The same remarks are applicable to Dr. C.'s attempt to identify the testimony of Irenæus with the passages which he has marked as specially observable under the name of Ignatius It must first be proved that Irenæus ever saw them This foundation of the argument must be established before the superstructure can stand.

But let us now review the evidence which these early fathers furnish *against* the system of Dr. C. For, as has been already observed, even the epistles of Ignatius in this respect are not supposed to have been interpolated; since, for this the state and progress of ecclesiastical affairs in the following ages evidently furnish no probable motive, as they plainly did for such freedoms on the opposite side.

Before I proceed to this, however, I beg leave to remind the reader that there was one other earlier Christian father, after the apostles, of whose writings Dr. C. seems content to make but little use. I mean Clemens Romanus—Clement of Rome. The writings of this father are characterized by Dr. Campbell as "the most respectable remains we have of Christian antiquity, next to the inspired writings." He then proceeds thus: "The piece I allude to is the first epistle of Clemens Romanus to the Corinthians, as it is commonly styled, but as it styles itself, 'The Epistle of the Church of God at Rome to the Church of God at Corinth' It is the same Clement whom Paul (Philip iv, 3) calls his fellow-labourer, and one of those whose names are in the book of life. There we are told, chap xlii, that 'the apostles, having preached the gospel in countries and towns, constituted the first-fruits of their ministry, whom they approved by the Spirit, bishops and deacons of those who should believe' And in order to satisfy us that he did not use these words in a vague manner, for church officers in general, but as expressive of all the distinct orders that were established by them in the church, he adds 'Nor was this a new device, inasmuch as bishops and deacons had been pointed out many ages before,—for thus says the Scripture, "*I will constitute their bishops in righteousness, and their deacons in faith*"' The passage quoted is the last clause of the 17th verse of the 60th chapter of Isaiah   It is thus rendered in our version . 'I will make thine officers peace, and thine exactors righteousness.'   Whether this venerable ancient has given a just translation, or made a proper application of this prediction, is not the point in question ; it is enough that it evinces what his notion was of the established ministers then in the church And if (as no critic ever questioned, and as his own argument necessarily requires,) he means the same by bishops with those who in the Acts are called πρεσβυτεροι, whom the apostles Paul and Barnabas ordained in every church, and whom Clement in other parts of this epistle also calls πρεσβυτεροι,—namely, the ordinary teachers ; it would seem strange that the bishop, properly so called, the principal officer of all, should be the only one in his account of whom the Holy Spirit, in sacred writ, had given no previous intimation.   Nay, do not the words of this father manifestly imply that any other office in the church than the two he had mentioned, might be justly styled a *new device* or invention? Dr Pearson, in his Vindiciæ Ignatianæ, insists much that whenever any of the fathers purposely enumerate the different orders in the church, they mention always three   If the above account given by Clement is not to be considered an enumeration, I know not what to call it.   If two were actually all the orders then in the church, could he have introduced the mention of them by telling us he was about to give a list or catalogue, or even to make an enumeration of the ecclesiastical degrees? Is this a way of prefacing the mention of so small a number as two? It is this writer's express design to acquaint us what the apostles did for accommodating the several churches they planted, in pastors and assistants And can we suppose he would have omitted the chief point of all, namely, that they supplied every church with a prelate, ruler, or head, if any one had really been entitled to this distinction?

"If it should be urged that under the term $\epsilon\pi\iota\sigma\kappa\sigma\pi\sigma\iota$, both functions of bishop and presbyter are comprehended, it is manifest that, as it was the writer's scope to mark the different offices established as being predicted by the prophets in the Old Testament, there cannot be a stronger indication that there was then no material, if any, difference between them, and that they were properly denominated and considered as one office The appellatives also by which they are denoted, are invariably employed by him in the plural number as being equally applicable to all It is said in chap i, $\tau\sigma\iota\varsigma$ $\eta\gamma\sigma\nu\mu\epsilon\nu\sigma\iota\varsigma$ $\dot{\nu}\mu\omega\nu$ $\dot{\nu}\tau\sigma\tau\alpha\sigma\sigma\sigma\mu\epsilon\nu\sigma\iota$, submitting to your governors or guides It is remarkable also that the word $\eta\gamma\sigma\nu\mu\epsilon\nu\sigma\varsigma$, here used in the plural of all their pastors, is one of those terms which came afterward to be appropriated to the bishop Nay, since it must be admitted, that in the New Testament, as well as in the ancient Christian monument just now quoted, the words $\epsilon\pi\iota\sigma\kappa\sigma\pi\sigma\varsigma$ and $\pi\rho\epsilon\nu\beta\nu\tau\epsilon\rho\sigma\varsigma$ are not occasionally, but uniformly, used synonymously; the very discovery that there was not any distinctive appellation for such an office as is now called bishop is not of inconsiderable weight to prove that it did not exist. We know that every other office, ordinary and extraordinary, is sufficiently distinguished by an appropriated name

"But I cannot help observing further concerning this

epistle of Clement, that though it was written with the special view of conciliating the minds of the Corinthians to their pastors, commonly in this letter called presbyters, some of whom the people had turned out of their offices, or expelled (απο της επισκοπης) from their bishoprick, as his words literally imply, there is not the most distant hint of any superior to these πρεσβυτεροι, whose proper province it was, if there had been such a superior, to inspect their conduct and to judge of it, and whose authority the people had treated most contemptuously, in presuming, without so much as consulting him, to degrade their presbyters   It was natural, it was even unavoidable, to take notice in such a case of the usurpation whereof they had been guilty upon their bishop— the chief shepherd, who had the oversight of all the under shepherds, the presbyters as well as of the people, and to whom alone, if there had been such a person, those presbyters were accountable for their conduct. Yet there is not so much as a syllable in all this long letter that points this way.   On the contrary, he argues from the power with which those presbyters themselves were vested, and of which they could not be justly stripped whilst they discharged faithfully the duties of their office.   1 will appeal to any candid person who is tolerably conversant in the Christian antiquities, whether he thinks it possible that in the third century such a letter, on such an emergence, could have been written to any Christian congregation by any man in his senses, wherein there was no more notice taken of the bishop, who was then, in a manner, every thing in his own church, than if he were nothing at all.   And that there was so great a difference, in less than two centuries, in people's style and sentiments on this article, is an uncontrovertible proof that in that period things came to stand on a very different foot   This epistle of Clement, who was a disciple of Paul, appears indeed from one passage to have been written so early as before the destruction of the temple at Jerusalem, and consequently before the seventy-second year of Christ, according to the vulgar computation   And if so, it was written before the Apocalypse, and perhaps some other parts of the sacred canon   Nothing, therefore, that is not Scripture, can be of greater authority in determining a point of fact, as is the question about the constitution of the apostolical church "*

It is proper to note here, that Dr Campbell afterward adds a general observation, to which he invites the attention of the judicious and candid, that what he has advanced does not affect the lawfulness, or even, in certain circumstances, the expediency of the episcopal model; but only exposes the arrogance of pretending to a *jus divinum,* [a divine right]   He is satisfied (as he continues, with a manly and Christian frankness worthy of all commendation and of more general imitation) that no form of polity can plead such an exclusive charter as that phrase, in its present acceptation, is understood to imply,—that the claim is clearly the offspring of sectarian bigotry and ignorance —That in regard to those polities which obtain at present in the different Christian sects, he ingenuously owns that he has not found one of all that he has examined, which can be said perfectly to coincide with the model of the apostolic church.   Some indeed are nearer, and some are more remote ; but this we may say with freedom, that if a particular form of polity had been essential to the church, it would have been laid down in a different manner in the sacred books —That the very hypothesis, in his opinion, is repugnant to the spiritual nature of the evangelical economy, and savours grossly of the conceit with which the Jews were intoxicated of the Messiah's secular kingdom,—a conceit with which many like-minded Christians are intoxicated still †

* Lectures, pp. 70–72   † Ib , pp. 73, 74.

Let it be observed also, that I quote Dr Campbell freely, not because I agree with him in all respects, but because, in the main points in this controversy, as between high church and us, his able work fully sustains our views as above stated.

I now return to Ignatius. In speaking of his epistles Dr C remarks, p 18, that "in every instance the bishop is mentioned in such terms as show that he was *the only one* in the church addressed" This Dr C marks emphatically, as is here done   The assertion is a very extraordinary one, and, I suppose, cannot have been intended to convey the meaning which the face of it imports.   For if the reader will turn to the epistles, he will find, on the contrary, that "in every instance," except the epistle to Polycarp, it is "the church" that is addressed   And although Dr. C. maintains that without a bishop, such as he describes, there is no church, yet I am not aware that he has yet taken upon himself to assert that the bishop alone is "the church"

But, passing this obscure passage, as perhaps merely wanting in felicity of expression, is it not singular that Ignatius, in addressing Polycarp, himself a bishop, and a disciple of St John, should say to him, *"Hearken unto the bishop, that God also may hearken unto you My soul be security for them that submit to their bishop, with their presbyters and deacons."* Yet so Dr. C. cites him, and this is one of the passages which he specially marks with Italics, as above.*   The passage itself, in such an epistle, is foisted as impertinently as the language is profane, and the sentiment antichristian

Dr C refers to Dr. Miller, as observing that several of the early fathers "expressly represent *presbyters* as the successors of the apostles : among others *Ignatius*" And afterward adds, " The reader may easily determine how far this assertion is correct, by turning to the

* Appendix, p xxiv.

passages in *Italic letters,* in the appendix to these pages "*

Well, I have done so .—confining myself to the passages marked by Dr C. himself. And what does the reader suppose is the result? Is he at all prepared to anticipate that several of these very passages expressly confirm Dr. Miller's assertion? If, considering the boldness with which Dr C. makes the reference, he deem this incredible, then I assure him that I quote them as they stand in Dr. C.'s own appendix, and as marked by himself; except that I put in small capitals the words which represent presbyters as successors of the apostles, which Dr. C leaves in Italics, in common with the rest of the passage.

In the epistle to the Magnesians, sect. 6, Ignatius says, "*I exhort you that ye study to do all things in divine concord · your bishop presiding in the place of God,* YOUR PRESBYTERS IN THE PLACE OF THE COUNCIL OF THE APOSTLES, *and your deacons most dear to me being intrusted with the ministry of Jesus Christ* "†

In the epistle to the Trallians, sect 2, he says, "*For whereas ye are subject to your bishop, as to Jesus Christ, ye appear to me to live not after the manner of men, but according to Jesus Christ   It is therefore necessary, that as ye do, so without your bishop you should do nothing ·* ALSO, BE YE SUBJECT TO YOUR PRESBYTERS, AS TO THE APOSTLES OF JESUS CHRIST OUR HOPE; *in whom if we walk, we shall be found in him   The deacons also, as being the ministers of the mysteries of Jesus Christ.*"‡

Again . in the same epistle to the Trallians, sect 3, he says . "*In like manner let all reverence the deacons as Jesus Christ, and the bishop as the Father, and* THE PRESBYTERS AS THE SANHEDRIM OF GOD, AND COLLEGE OF THE APOSTLES "‡

In the epistle to the Smyrneans, he says : "*See that*

---

* Dr C. p. 19.   † Appendix, p x   ‡ Ib , p xii

ye all follow your bishop, as Jesus Christ, the Father; and THE PRESBYTERY AS THE APOSTLES, *and reverence the deacons as the command of God*"*

An examination of the above passages may aid the reader in forming a judgment of the incautiousness, to use no stronger term, with which Dr. C. makes the most positive and extraordinary affirmations Of that cited above from the 6th section of the epistle to the Magnesians, he says, "Take the whole together, and the meaning is precisely the reverse of that which Dr Miller represents it to be," p 19 Now Dr Miller's statement was, that Ignatius in that passage represents *presbyters* as the successors of the apostles This then, at present, is the single question; and Dr. C. must be held to it Does that whole passage of Ignatius, taken together, represent presbyters as the successors of the apostles, or does it represent "precisely the reverse?" The former is Dr Miller's assertion, the latter is Dr C's I leave the reader, after looking back at the passage, to judge between them

Dr. C. himself, indeed, very soon afterward, p. 20, seems smitten with the conviction that Ignatius does "represent the presbyters as standing in the place of the apostles" For he there adds, (after mentioning Dr Miller's farther quotation of the 3d section of the epistle to the Trallians also,) " If these passages represent the presbyters as standing in the place of the apostles, they place the bishop as far above them as he could by any language be represented to be." I grant it.—even as far—I pause, and am shocked to repeat such language,—yes, even as far as GOD is above the apostles ! Certainly language cannot go higher. It is indeed, reader, a sober verity. Dr. C. himself, a little after, on the same page, repeats with manifest approbation. "They represent the bishop as standing in the place of God."

* Appendix, p xxii.

Such then is a Christian bishop, according to the epistles of Ignatius, which Dr C pronounces "most unexceptionable ," and such, consequently, in the judgment of Dr C , is a Christian bishop still, "standing in the place of God, as far above presbyters,—and certainly, of course, above deacons, laics, and the whole church beside his single self,—as God above the apostles !" If deeds of ineffable atrocity may be expressed as outheroding Herod, surely the challenging of such insufferable, even infinite pre-eminence for the episcopal dignity and authority, may not inappositely be branded as outpoping (if I may coin this term for the special occasion) the pope himself.

In truth, it is very far worse than popery. For, according to popery, there is but one supreme sovereign bishop, the absolute ruler of the whole church. But according to this scheme, each and every bishop is such within his diocese, of whatever extent. And thus the entire church of Christ on earth must be subjected, if this notion prevail, to the absolute domination of an unlimited number of popes, instead of one,—against whom, however arbitrary, partial, or oppressive their acts may be, there is no redress, and no appeal but to God *

In remarking on the writings of Cyprian, bishop of Carthage, about the middle of the third century, Dr. Jortin observes, that there are many passages in them containing high notions of episcopal authority and eccle-

---

* See Dr. Cook's draft of the episcopate of Bishop Timothy, the model by divine title, on his plan, of all succeeding bishops, p 8   In the Litany of the Church of England there was formerly this petition,—"*From the tyranny of the bishop of Rome, and all his detestable enormities, good Lord deliver us* " By order of Queen Elizabeth, who was somewhat tenderly concerned not to offend the pope, this passage was struck out   But surely Protestants of the present day may most rationally, most scripturally, and most devoutly pray,—From an episcopal scheme, which claims by divine right the elevation of fallen, fallible men to such dignity and power above their fellow-men, their fellow-Christians, and their fellow-ministers, good Lord deliver us!

siastical jurisdiction   " While he strenuously opposed
the domination of one pope," continues the learned and
ingenious archdeacon, " he seemed in some manner to
make as many popes as bishops, and mere *arithmetical
naughts* of the rest of the Christians , which yet, I
believe," he adds, " was not his intent."*

Charity would lead us to hope as much of the *inten-
tions* of Dr C.

Whatever rank then Dr C may be disposed to assert
for such bishops as he contends for, if presbyters stand
in the place of the apostles, this is enough for us.   We
neither ask nor wish any thing more or higher.   And
whether this be not the explicit testimony of those epistles of Ignatius which Dr C avers to be genuine and
most unexceptionable, I shall submit to the judgment
of the reader, after laying before him the following
recapitulation of the specific clauses touching this point

" *Your presbyters in the place of the council of the
apostles* " Epistle to the Magnesians, sect. 6.

That is, as the preceding clause demonstrates, " your
presbyters [presiding] in the place of the council of the
apostles "

" *Also be ye subject to your presbyters as to the apostles of Jesus Christ our hope* " Epistle to the Trallians,
sect 2

" *And the presbyters as the sanhedrim of God, and
college of the apostles* " *Ib* , sect 3

That is, as the context shows, Let all reverence the
presbyters as the sanhedrim of God, and college of the
apostles

" *And the presbytery as the apostles* " Epistle to the
Smyrneans, sect 8

That is, as the context here also demonstrates, See
that ye all follow the presbytery as the apostles

I remark here by the way, and shall have occasion to

---

* Remarks on Ecclesiastical History, vol 1, p 415.

notice it again, that by the "presbytery," in this place, is incontestably meant—not an office—but the body of presbyters, as contradistinguished from the bishop and the deacons, severally, and from them both together. The reader will please bear in mind this ancient use of the term by an apostolical father, as Dr C contends, a disciple of the apostles, and so near the apostolic age. It will be important in the argument in another place.

It may be proper also to observe at this stage, that it is not my purpose, or my place, to volunteer in the vindication of Dr Miller In the main point,—the validity of ordination by presbyters,—that eminent divine and we entirely agree. In others we differ, and, I trust, agree to differ; neither of us regarding a difference of judgment or practice in matters of polity, a sufficient occasion for schism among Christians, in the true Scriptural sense of this term, but still recognising the communion of each other as within the covenant mercies of the Father of mercies, and the comprehensive pale of the catholic church *

I may be permitted here also to say, that a very large portion of Dr C 's authorities and arguments against the Presbyterian scheme of parity, as advocated by Dr Miller, are entirely irrelevant and harmless, as will hereafter be shown,† in regard to the Methodist Episcopal polity, which recognises both an order of bishops, officially superior to presbyters, and the order of deacons as ministers of Christ

In combating Dr Miller, Dr. C occasionally avails himself of a reference to Methodist usages, to help out his argument For example ·—from the language of Ignatius to Polycarp, bishop of Smyrna, charging him to let his assemblies be more full,—to inquire into all by name,—and not to overlook the men or maid ser-

* See note B, Appendix [Never written —Ed]

† [This the author probably designed to do in the second part of his Essay, which, as has been already stated, was never written —Ed.]

vants; Dr Miller contends that the bishop of that day was the pastor of a single church, and not a diocesan in the modern sense Dr C answers, " This can be done without personal acquaintance The preachers of the Methodist travelling connection on many circuits have above a thousand, and on some twelve or fourteen hundred persons under their care, sometimes spread over circuits of fifty or sixty miles in extent, and they inquire *into all by name,*—not overlooking the men and maid servants,—*every four weeks* "* This is certainly a high compliment to us I only wish it were strictly merited

But if our economy,—may I say, without seeming to assume too much, our excellent economy,—helps Dr C. out in one instance, does not justice require that Dr. Miller should have the benefit of it in another? for it is in truth a middle ground, which certainly solves very many of the difficulties between the two extremes, and on which the contending parties might happily meet, were there mutually that disposition to Christian concord which we should be happy to see prevail. Dr C. says, for example, in another place, that if Dr Miller could establish one of his statements alluded to, " he would make a difficulty which he would find it not easy to solve. For no presbyter, the pastor of a church, has a presbytery, or council of presbyters, *in his church,* who are his brothers and *colleagues* "†

Now, if Dr C or Dr M will look again into the usage of the Methodist Episcopal Church, they will find an easy solution of that difficulty also. The very thing alleged by Dr. C. as never existing, exists at this moment among us, in New-York, in Baltimore, in Charleston, in Cincinnati, and in many other places which might be named

The next ancient Christian writer to whose testimony

* Page 26   † Page 79.

reference is made in this controversy, is *Polycarp* *
Dr. C. indeed seems not to have found much in this
father to his purpose, although he wrote after Ignatius,
and consequently might be expected to speak still more
strongly on the distinction of the three orders, if it then
existed, since it is well known that after it once obtained
footing it never retrograded, but steadily advanced till
the completion of the entire hierarchal structure

It is true, as I have before remarked, that Dr. C.
claims the testimony of Polycarp as identical with that
of Ignatius, in consequence of some general expressions of the former in regard to the epistles, and the
personal worth of the latter. In answer to this, I have
above said that all the arguments which go to disprove
the genuineness, or at least the integrity, of the epistles
ascribed to Ignatius, serve equally to render it at least
entirely uncertain whether Polycarp ever saw them as
we now have them, and especially those very passages
on which Dr C mainly relies, which are especially suspicious, and consequently cannot be fairly made the
ground of any certain argument But, even supposing
it otherwise : then, according to Dr C 's own showing,
we have the additional testimony of Polycarp that
presbyters stand in the place of the apostles In proof
of which I refer the reader to the quotations made
above, from Dr. C 's own edition of Ignatius's epistles
And this, I repeat, concedes all that we have the slightest inclination even to ask in the argument

Dr C urges the fact that if the epistles of Ignatius
" represent the presbyters as standing in the place of the
apostles, they place the bishop as far above them as
he could by any language be represented to be :" p. 20
What, then, will he say to the testimony of Polycarp,
who, throughout his whole epistle to the Philippians,

* Dr Miller places Polycarp in chronological order before Ignatius. Dr.
Campbell, however, more correctly I think, remarks that the writings of
Ignatius are supposed to have preceded those of Polycarp Lectures, p 73

4

speaks of two orders only of ministers, viz, presbyters and deacons, never even naming that of bishop,—but, on the contrary, enjoining the people to be subject to their presbyters and deacons as to God and Christ. Could he, by any language, have represented any order higher than this? and had he known any order in the church then superior to that of the presbyters, to which they themselves owed subjection, could he, even decently, have adopted the highest possible similitude to illustrate the obedience due to *their* order? Nay, farther, when in the same epistle he lays down the duties and qualifications of deacons and presbyters, wherein every thing befitting judges and governors is included, and those of the people also throughout the epistle, is it not unaccountable that he should never even mention or allude to what was proper on the part of the higher order, or on the part of the presbyters, deacons, and people, toward such higher order, if he knew of any such then existing? Let common sense answer these questions *

* A specimen of the facility with which Dr C. begs a question, when he can find no more logical mode of settling it, is furnished in a remark which he makes respecting Polycarp, p 84. He had just observed that Dr Miller roundly admits, in the outset of his reference to this father, that Polycarp speaks of two orders of ministers, and then adds,—"and when we know that he himself belonged to a third" Now does not Dr C "know" that this is the very point in debate? Yet nothing is more common than such dogmatizing throughout his book Another similar instance just strikes my eye, near the same place, p 85 He had just referred again to what is alleged from Ignatius, "in support of the three orders," and then adds, "that we could not have any thing of an opposite character from Polycarp, *is evident from the circumstance of his being himself bishop of the church at Smyrna, with presbyters under him*" Is evident! In what school of logic has such arguing been learned? If the simple fact that Polycarp was bishop, superintendent, overseer, or rector of the church at Smyrna, with presbyters under him, proves conclusively that he was therefore necessarily of a third order of ministers, by divine right, inherently and essentially distinct from and superior to the order of presbyters, then the controversy is ended But surely it cannot be necessary to remind the reader, if it be to remind Dr C., that this is still the precise point in dispute. The very same sophism is used by Dr C on the next page (86) in regard to Clement I will only add here, that the whole of his effort, pp 84, 85, to account consistently with his (Dr C's) scheme, for Polycarp's omission of

4*

I cannot say, with Dr C, that I think the representing of any order in the church as standing in the place
of God, or the reverence and obedience due to it, by
that which we owe to the Almighty, "most unexceptionable." For my own part, I humbly think such comparisons, whether in Ignatius or in Polycarp, very
exceptionable But then, if one early father thought
proper to use them in reference to bishops, and another,
his contemporary, who was also an apostolical father,
and the disciple of an apostle, did so in like manner in
reference to presbyters, is not the argument from their
authority and language quite as good in the latter case
as in the former ?

In regard to the form of polity, however, the fact is,
that the epistles of Ignatius and Polycarp, as we have
them, cannot both, as Dr Campbell remarks, be made
applicable to the same state of the church

The difference between them is not a diversity in
style, but a repugnance in sentiment. so that we are
forced to conclude that in the writings of one or the
other there must have been something spurious or interpolated. "Now," continues the same able critic, "I
have heard no argument used against the authenticity
of Polycarp's letter equally cogent as some of the arguments employed against the authenticity of the epistles
of Ignatius And, indeed, the state of the church, in no
subsequent period, can well account for such a forgery
as the epistle of the former to the Philippians ; whereas
the ambition of the ecclesiastics, for which some of the
following centuries were remarkable, renders it extremely easy to account for the nauseous repetition of

any mention whatever throughout his epistle, of any such superior third
order, is totally overthrown by his using the highest similitude possible, as
above stated, to illustrate the order of presbyters and the obedience due to
them, a similitude, certainly, which he could not with any propriety, or
even decency, have applied to this order, had he known any higher in the
church

obedience and subjection to the bishop, presbyters, and deacons, to be found in the letters of Ignatius."*

I may add here, that *Irenæus*, who is the next of the ancient fathers introduced, testifies of Polycarp, who, as Irenæus affirms, was taught by the apostles, and conversed with many of those who had seen our Lord, that "he always taught those things which he had learned from the apostles, which he likewise delivered to the church, and which are alone true" Book iii, chap. 3, *Against Heresies.* In the same paragraph he particularly mentions the "most excellent epistle of Polycarp to the Philippians, above cited, from which," he adds, "they who wish and have regard for their own salvation, can learn the character of his faith, and the doctrine of the truth"

Such then were Polycarp's views of church order, at least in the apostolical Philippian church, and such Irenæus's commendation of the "most excellent epistle" containing them.

The objection that Polycarp was himself a bishop, will be noticed hereafter I now proceed to *Irenæus.*

At what precise time Irenæus wrote, authors are not agreed Dr Campbell says he is supposed to have written about the middle of the second century Lord King places him about the year 184 And Dr Miller says he is said to have suffered martyrdom about the year 202. For this even Dr C. adopts the same date, p 81 How long it was before his martyrdom that his work against heresies was written, does not appear. There is one passage in the third book, however, which strongly inclines me to adopt the latest of the dates assigned for him It is that in which he mentions as a thing observable, that when he was a youth he himself had seen Polycarp; and states at the same time that Polycarp attained a very great age before his martyrdom. Now the date assigned for Polycarp's writings

* Lectures on Ecclesiastical History, p 97.

by Lord King is the year 140, and it is probable that they were at least not much earlier; and if so, then that those of Irenæus did not appear till considerably after the middle of the second century, and probably not till toward the latter part of it Now it is acknowledged that by that time a distinction between bishop and presbyters, as of different orders, began to prevail, although it was much less considerable than it became afterward This fact, therefore, may reasonably be supposed to have influenced the style of Irenæus's writings, and accounts for the difference in this respect between him and Polycarp.

In regard to the character of Irenæus, and the weight due to his testimony, I wish not to detract from it. Yet, as in all other uninspired human compositions, so also in those of the ancient Christian writers in particular, due allowance must be made for the time and the circumstances in which they wrote, which had a pervading influence both on their turn of thought and their style of expression. And in regard to Irenæus himself, notwithstanding Mosheim's commendation of the " erudition' of his books against heresies, for that is the amount of it, another very eminent critic, himself an Episcopalian—I mean Archdeacon Jortin—says of that ancient father, " I fear it will be no very easy task to clear him entirely from the imputation of credulity and inaccuracy "*

Dr. C, moreover, seems to suppose, or leaves his readers to suppose, that Irenæus wrote in *Latin;* and hence he appends to his own work the third chapter of the third book of Irenæus against heresies in Latin, without stating that this not only was not the original, but that, even as a *translation,* it is pronounced by an able judge to be *excessively barbarous* †

* Remarks on Ecclesiastical History, vol. i, p 363

† See Dr Maclaine's note, Mosheim, vol i, p. 177.

In introducing his quotations from Irenæus, Dr C says, "The following is a translation of the third chapter of the third of those books Against Heresies—" * Would not readers generally infer from this, that he meant a translation from the original? Whereas, if he would not make an erroneous impression, he should have said,—The following is a translation of a translation. to which, on the authority of Dr. Maclaine, I add, and that an excessively barbarous one.

Dr Miller makes a quotation from the fourth book of Irenæus, ch xliv, which is rendered thus "We ought therefore to adhere to *those presbyters who keep the apostles' doctrine*, and together with the *presbyterial succession*, do show forth sound speech Such presbyters the church nourishes; and of such the prophet says, I will give them *princes* in peace, and *bishops in righteousness*." In his criticisms on this quotation, Dr. Cooke says, " The passage runs thus in Irenæus: 'Adhærere vero his qui,"' &c. †   Would not readers generally most fairly and reasonably infer from this, that Dr. C meant to convey the idea that these were the identical words of Irenæus himself? It may not be amiss then to inform such that this is altogether a mistake; Irenæus did not write in Latin at all, but in *Greek*. and that we have not even an opportunity to compare the barbarous Latin of his translator, in this part of the work, with the original, since the first book only of Irenæus is extant in the original Greek, the rest being preserved to us only in the barbarous Latin translation. Yet on this Dr C would build criticisms and inferences of such immense importance to the very being of the Christian church! I pray thee have us excused.

But I will take Dr. C. on his own criticism. The phrase " *cum presbyteri ordine*," from the Latin transla-

* Page 71,   † Page 76, *note.*

tion of Irenæus, is rendered in Dr Miller's quotation, " with *the presbyterial succession.*" Now, says Dr C, " To bear this signification, there should be an adjective to agree with *ordine,* or the noun should be in the plural, *presbyterorum* As it stands, it can only mean something belonging to a presbyter. We frequently meet with the expression *successiones episcoporum,* not *episcopi* · so, if this passage meant presbyterial succession, or a succession of presbyters, the word used would have been *presbyterorum,* not *presbyteri.*"* Well, let us take, then, the following passage from the same Latin translation of Irenæus, and apply his own rule to it :— " Cum autem ad eam iterum traditionem quæ est ab apostolis quæ *per successiones presbyterorum* in ecclesiis custoditur, provocamus eos, qui adversantur traditioni, dicent se non solum presbyteris, sed etiam apostolis existentes sapientiores, synceram invenisse veritatem " Lib. iii, cap 2 Here we have the precise phrase " *successiones presbyterorum,*" which, according to Dr C. himself, means *presbyterial succession* Indeed, if " *successiones episcoporum*" means *episcopal succession,* as he contends, then " *successiones presbyterorum,*" by his own rule, must mean *presbyterial succession* He must inevitably admit both or give up both, or renounce all pretensions to candour in criticism

Let it be especially noted here, also, that in the above cited passage from Irenæus, not only are the *successions of presbyters* mentioned as the channel through which the apostolic tradition [whether of doctrine or order] had been preserved in the churches, but no notice whatever is taken of any superior order ; an omission, which, had there been any such of the distinct supreme rank which Dr. C alleges for bishops, would, to say the least, have been extremely unbecoming, and would argue very little in favour of the accuracy of the author.

* Page 76.

Granting then that the phrase "*successiones episcopo-rum*" is also to be met with,—what does this prove? It proves precisely what we believe to be the true and candid view of the subject. that is to say, that even down to the time of Irenæus, and to the end of that century, either no difference of order was considered as existing between presbyters and bishops, or the difference was regarded as so small and unessential, that these titles were frequently interchanged by the writers of those times In fact, as Dr. Campbell affirms, and as the above passage plainly shows, Irenæus talks in much the same style of both What at one time he ascribes to bishops, at another he ascribes to presbyters. He speaks of each as entitled to obedience from the people, as succeeding the apostles in the ministry, and as *the succession* through which the apostolic doctrine and tradition had been handed down

That the names bishop and presbyter are often inter-changed by Irenæus, as well as other writers of his time, even to the end of the century, is admitted by the learned *Bishop Pearson*, who, however, maintains that this happened only when they spoke of the ministry in general terms, or mentioned those ministers only who had preceded them; affirming that, in regard to their own contemporaries, the offices of individuals are never thus confounded Dr Campbell admits the truth of this remark, and considers it a very strong confirm-ation of the doctrine here defended For what rea-sonable account can be given of this manner (other-wise chargeable with the most unpardonable inaccu-racy) but by saying that in the time of the predecessors of Irenæus there was no material distinction of order between bishops and presbyters; whereas in his own time the distinction began to be marked by peculiar powers and prerogatives If this had not been the case, it was as little natural as excusable to be less accurate in speaking of those that went before, than of those in his own time   Was it ever observed of writers in the fourth and fifth centuries, to come no lower, that they in this manner confounded the different ecclesiastical offices of the third?   Is Cyprian, for instance, in any succeeding age, styled a presbyter of Carthage, or Rogatian the bishop?   Are not their respective titles as uniformly observed in after ages as in their own?*

In regard to the passage above mentioned, as cited by Dr. Miller from Irenæus, book iv, chap xliv, on which Dr C founds his criticism respecting the presbyterial succession, which I have just discussed, he subsequently adds as follows: "For the whole amount of it, as it stands, is, To such presbyters (as with the discipline of a presbyter show forth sound speech, &c.) I will give *princes* in peace, and *bishops* in righteousness. Certainly" [continues Dr C.] "it would not appear from this form of expression that the presbyter was the bishop"†

Whether this observation be solid or merely specious may be tested by an allusion to the same place of the prophet, by another *more ancient* and more immediately *apostolical father*,—I mean Clement, whose testimony I have before adduced   This father, in his epistle to the Corinthians, before mentioned, states, chap xlii, that "the apostles, having preached the gospel in countries and towns, constituted the first-fruits of their ministry, whom they approved by the Spirit, bishops and deacons of those who should believe"   And to show that he did not use these words vaguely, but as expressive of the distinct orders established by the apostles in the churches, he adds, "Nor was this a new device. inasmuch as bishops and deacons had been pointed out many ages before ; for thus says the Scripture, 'I will constitute their bishops in righteousness and their dea-

* Lectures on Ecclesiastical History, pp 100, 101.
† Pages 76, 77.

cons in faith.' "* The passage alluded to is Isaiah
lx, 17 Whether Clement's translation or application
of it be correct is not now in question It is enough
for our present purpose that it shows clearly, not only
what his opinion but what his knowledge was of the
orders of ministers constituted by the apostles in the
churches which they planted ; for to do this was his
express design Those whom in this passage he calls
bishops, in other parts of the same epistle he calls presbyters, demonstrating thereby that he uses the two terms
interchangeably, as expressive of one and the same
order. And most indisputably he speaks of but *two*
orders in the apostolical churches, constituted by the
apostles themselves ; at the same time that his express
object was to state the ministerial orders in the churches
thus constituted If, then, we interpret Irenæus by
Clement, a more ancient father, and the fellow-labourer
of St Paul himself, we must say, in contradiction of
Dr. C., that it would appear from his form of expression,—Clement being interpreter,—both that the bishop
was a presbyter, and that a presbyter was the bishop ;
in a word, that the ministerial degrees in the apostolical churches consisted of *two orders* only, whether
called bishops and deacons, or presbyters and deacons
Keeping this in view, as placed in this clear light by
the venerable Clement, there remains no difficulty whatever, on the principles of the Methodist Episcopal polity,
in any part of the whole third chapter of the third book
of Irenæus, or in any other quotation from that father,
even as given in the translation of a translation, furnished by Dr C

Dr C. himself thus sums up his own view of the
strongest points, extracted from Irenæus

"1 That the apostles appointed bishops in all the

---

* So the passage from Clement is rendered in Campbell's Lectures,
p. 70.

churches, and left them as their successors TO GOVERN THE CHURCH.

2. That the episcopate or bishopric was delivered to one person, and one bishop only *at a time*, is ever mentioned as governing the church: thus the apostles delivered the episcopate to Linus, *to govern the church* at Rome; Anacletus *succeeded* him, and *after him*, in the third place, Clement obtained the episcopate, and the names of twelve *successive* bishops are given, who governed that church, each in his day, as indicated by the expressions, *under Clement, under Anicetus*

3 It is expressly stated that there were successions of bishops *in all the churches*, and that with the church at Rome, in which the names of twelve successive bishops are given, every church should agree, that is, *those which were in all respects faithful*

4 That Polycarp was taught by the apostles, and was *by them appointed bishop of Smyrna* "*

Again "Irenæus says," [continues Dr C] "True knowledge is the doctrine of the apostles, &c *according to the successions of the bishops, to whom they* (viz, the apostles) *delivered that church which is in every place*," &c †

And again "In the twentieth chapter of the fifth book, speaking of those who derive their authority from the apostles, in comparison with heretics, he says, 'For they are all far behind *the bishops to whom the apostles delivered the churches*, and this we have with all carefulness made apparent in the third book'"†

Now in all the above, there is nothing whatever in the slightest manner incompatible with the inherent identity of the order of bishops and presbyters, as the existing polity and usage of the Methodist Episcopal Church, which give to the bishops official superiority among their fellow-presbyters and in the government of the churches, especially illustrate This any intel-

* Page 73.　　　† Page 74.

ligent and candid person who will take the pains to look into them may readily perceive and perfectly understand For it has been proved from Clement, as above, that those whom the apostles constituted bishops in the churches which they planted, and whom they left their successors, delivering to them their own place of government, were of that order of ministers next above deacons, whom Clement sometimes calls bishops and at other times presbyters, and that no other intervening order whatever is mentioned or alluded to throughout his whole epistle If Irenæus therefore does not contradict Clement, we must so understand him also ; and if he does contradict him, then Clement is the better authority of the two

But that Irenæus does in fact agree with Clement, there seems to me very plain and positive proof In his fourth book, chap. xliii he speaks of "those presbyters in the church who have the succession, as he had shown, from the apostles ; who, *with the succession of the episcopate,* received the gift of truth, according to the good pleasure of the Father " This passage Dr C. does not dispute ; but makes the following very just comment on it " That Irenæus was here speaking of bishops is concluded from the word ' episcopate,' and from the reference to what he had said before "* Very true This is exactly our own opinion And hence it follows incontestably, according to this authority, that the true succession from the apostles, and " the succession of the episcopate" itself, is with presbyters, one of them at a time, within his charge, whether less or more, being vested with official superiority in the government of his fellow-ministers and the churches, and yet being intrinsically and inherently but a presbyter among presbyters,—though occupying the first seat and the first official degree, both in dignity and

* Page 77

authority, as the speaker of the House of Commons, in Great Britain, who, nevertheless, is still inherently but a commoner among commoners.

Dr C. himself, indeed, is compelled to admit "that Irenæus sometimes uses the word presbyter in speaking of those who govern the churches, *qui præsunt ecclesiis* There are three other passages in which he does the same " *

Afterward, it is true, he makes an effort to neutralize this admission, on the principle that the apostles were sometimes called elders; and of the saying of Hilary, "The bishop is the chief,—though every bishop is a presbyter, yet every presbyter is not a bishop" Very true This again is exactly our own opinion. And it proves, according to Hilary also, that though *every* presbyter is not a bishop, yet that *some* presbyters *are* bishops; for this is evidently the drift of the saying Nor is this in the slightest measure contradicted by what Irenæus says in other places "of the church [of Rome, for example] being governed by the bishop, BY ONE BISHOP AT A TIME," or of those whose names he mentions in succession, "who *singly* governed the church, *each in his day*" On the plan of the Methodist Episcopal polity, presbyters do govern the churches "in the sense in which the word *præsunt* is used" And whether the term be applied to our bishops as general superintendents, or even to presiding elders within their districts, or to our ordinary presbyters in charge of circuits or stations in which there may be "many thousands of Christians and numerous presbyters." still it may be strictly said of them, "*qui præsunt ecclesiis*,"—who preside in or over the churches.

The "most explicit passage on this subject," in the letter of Irenæus to Victor, bishop of Rome, admits of exactly the same solution. And on a careful review of

* Page 77.

what has been said, I now repeat the assertion of Dr.
Campbell, and what he states has been admitted by
Bishop Pearson, that the names bishop and presbyter
are often interchanged by Irenæus, to which I add,
that this interchangeable use of them, as essentially the
same order, alone reconciles him both to himself and to
that still more venerable ancient, *Clemens Romanus*,
who being among the first bishops of Rome itself, the
very pattern and model of all other churches, according
to Irenæus and Dr C, certainly understood the true,
apostolical order.

There remains one other "most explicit" passage,
adduced by Dr. Miller from the letter of Irenæus to
Victor, bishop of Rome, which I do, not perceive that
Dr C. has noticed. It is as follows —" Those *pres-*
byters before *Soter*, who *governed* the church, which thou
Victor, *now governest*, [the church of Rome,] I mean
Anicetus, *Pius*, *Hyyginus*, *Telesphorus*, and *Sixtus*, they
did not observe it . [he is speaking of the day of keeping *Easter*.] and those *presbyters who preceded you*,
though they did not observe it themselves, yet sent the
eucharist to those of other churches who did observe
it. And when blessed *Polycarp*, in the days of *Ani-*
cetus, came to *Rome,* he did not much persuade *Anicetus*
to observe it, as he (Anicetus) declared that the custom
of *the presbyters who were his predecessors* should be
retained " *

In this decisive passage, those who had "*singly*
governed the church [of Rome] *each in his day*," and
" in succession," before the time of Victor, who was
contemporary with Irenæus, probably between the
middle and close of the second century, are uniformly
styled *presbyters*. This seems to me a very strong
confirmation of the remark of Dr Campbell, on the
admission of Bishop Pearson above quoted, viz, that

* Miller's Letters, pp 152, 153

Irenæus, and other Christian writers of that century, used the names bishop and presbyter interchangeably, in reference to those who had preceded them, because the distinction of these church officers as two orders, although it began, perhaps, to be somewhat prevalent toward the middle of that century, yet had not, even to its close, become by any means so settled as it afterward did ; and hence the great difference observable in this respect between the style of the Christian writers of the fourth and fifth centuries, for example, to come no lower, and those of the second

It cannot be necessary to repeat, in answer to Dr C , what has so often been said, and is so perfectly obvious to the plainest understanding, that the attributing of superiority in government and official elevation to the individual presbyter constituted bishop, does not in the slightest degree invalidate the remark above made, or the argument founded on it. This is essential to our own hypothesis, and is exemplified both in fact and in language in our own ecclesiastical polity, now before the eyes of the whole community.

Before I introduce a quotation from another Christian father of the second century, I mean *Clemens Alexandrinus,* who flourished about the close of the century, I must remind the reader that confirmation, as well as ordination, is deemed by high churchmen as one of the peculiar acts of a bishop. Dr. Miller had quoted Clemens Alexandrinus as saying, in reference to the impropriety of women wearing false hair,—"On whom or what will the *presbyter* impose his hand ? To whom or what will he give his blessing ? Not to the woman who is adorned, but to strange locks of hair, and through them to another head " He had then remarked, that it is extremely doubtful whether Clement here alludes to confirmation at all, and that, if he does, it is the first hint in all antiquity of this rite being practised , and it is especially unfortunate for the high church cause

that Clement ascribes its performance to *presbyters.*
Dr C, however, admits it as a case of confirmation,
and says, p. 87, "Here a presbyter confirms, which
being (Dr. Miller argues) the office of a bishop, it is
evident that bishops and presbyters are one. To this
[continues Dr. C] it is replied, that in Egypt it was
the custom, *when the bishop was absent,* for the presbyters to confirm   '*Apud Ægyptum presbyteri confirmant,
si præsens non sit episcopus.*' This very exception [Dr.
Cook still continues] proves the rule, that it was
the bishop's special duty   It was only when he was
absent that the presbyters confirmed ; and moreover,
the statement that *in Egypt* this was the custom, implies
that it was not the common practice of the church." In
the greater part of this passage Dr. C speaks sensibly
and pertinently, and concedes, I think, every thing that
we need in the argument   Let it be especially noted
that he does not deny that confirmation, as well as ordination, is one of the peculiar acts of a bishop   And
then he admits that when the bishop was absent the
presbyter confirmed, although it was the bishop's special
duty when present   The latter I grant very freely.
But if in his absence the presbyter might perform acts
otherwise peculiar to him, then this proves that presbyters possess an inherent capacity for the legitimate performance of such acts,—although in churches episcopally constituted, they are, for the sake of order and
harmony, restrained by the custom or law of the church
from the performance of such acts where there is a
bishop   And this is all we ask   As to the remaining
observation of Dr C that "the statement that *in Egypt*
this was the custom, implies that it was not the common
practice of the church,'—I do not think that this is a
necessary consequence   It may be, that Clement, being
himself an Egyptian, meant to be understood as speaking of what was within his own knowledge, without
intending to affirm or deny any thing as to the practice

in other countries Analagous phrases, moreover, on other subjects, will show at once that Dr C.'s inference is not a necessary one from the premises If it be said, for example, that in America there are persons of all conditions, and a great diversity of soils and climates,— does it by any means follow that the speaker must necessarily be understood as affirming that this is not the case in any other quarter of the world? Clearly not No more, I think, is Dr C.'s inference a necessary one from the observation of Clement.

But be it, for argument's sake, that Clement so intended Still it is thus proved by his testimony, that *in Egypt* at least, at that early period, this was deemed a legitimate practice : and let it not be forgotten, that besides the many other churches in Egypt, there was that of Alexandria especially, one of the most famous of all the ancient churches, the seat of Christian letters and science, and, next after Rome, the greatest city in the ancient world That there may have been a diversity in some of the usages, and in the polity, in important respects, among the primitive churches even of apostolical plantation, seems highly probable, as well from this instance, according to Dr C 's own view of it, as from other considerations And this, too, is in perfect accordance with our principles

There is one decisive witness, however, whose testimony as to the general usage, even down to a much later period, wholly overthrows Dr C 's inference from the above passage of Clement The witness to whom I allude is *Jerome,* one of the most eminent Christian writers about the close of the fourth century and the beginning of the fifth. I shall hereafter have occasion for a much more particular reference to this father. At present, I merely wish to adduce that well-known passage in his famous letter to Evagrius ·—" Quid enim facit, excepta ordinatione, episcopus, quod presbyter non faciat?" "For what does a bishop which a presbyter

5

may not do, excepting ordination ?" In regard to ordination, the consideration of this passage will be resumed in another place. At present I confine myself to the point in hand, viz, confirmation   Does not Jerome expressly affirm in the above passage,—for the question is but a mode of strongly affirming,—that even in his time a bishop did nothing which a presbyter might not do, except ordaining? Nor does he affirm this as an " exception,"—as a thing limited to any particular place, —but as a well-known general fact, which would not then be disputed   Yet, plain as this is, and although Dr C himself, after Bowden, quotes this very passage in the English, to prove from Jerome that presbyters had not the right of ordaining, so obstinately is he bent on carrying his point, that in the very next paragraph, p 107, he undertakes to draw an inference from another passage in the same Jerome, also taken from Bowden, that bishops had the *exclusive* right of *confirmation* also! In other words, Jerome first says explicitly and positively, in the interrogatory form of affirmation, that a presbyter might do any thing a bishop did, except ordination , and Dr C himself quotes and urges this ; yet in the next breath draws an inference from a vague and ambiguous passage, that Jerome's testimony is, that confirmation is the exclusive prerogative of a bishop, as well as ordination, and that presbyters could perform neither ! What may not be forced from a witness if tortured in this way ?

Just as easy would it be, on this plan of managing testimony, to reconcile Tertullian, whom he next introduces, with what he alleges from Ignatius   The latter asserts, according to Dr. C , that where there is not a bishop, priest, and deacon, in his sense, *"there is no church"* And Tertullian affirms that where there was none of the clerical order, even laymen both celebrated the eucharist and baptized, and served as priests to themselves: for that *three persons, though laymen*, make a church.

5*

"Ubi ecclesiastici ordinis non est consessus, et offers, et tinguis, et sacerdos es tibi solus. Sed ubi tres, ecclesia est, licet laici "*

After the above extract, I should suppose that nothing more, certainly, can be necessary to demonstrate that Tertullian at least was not of the sect of high church. But Dr C. asserts, p. 91, that Tertullian and Irenæus "agree entirely." How then does he reconcile this with a former assertion that Irenæus agrees with what he alleges from Ignatius? For in regard to the essential constituents of a church, Tertullian and the alleged Ignatius are as diametrically at points as opposites can possibly be, and things agreeing with one and the same thing ought to agree with each other.

There is another passage of Tertullian in the following words : "Superest ad concludendam materiolam de observatione quoque dandi et accipiendi baptismum commonefacere Dandi quidem habet jus summus sacerdos, qui est episcopus. Dehinc presbyteri et diaconi ; non tamen sine episcopi auctoritate propter ecclesiæ honorem Quo salvo, salva pax est. Alioquin etiam laicis jus est "† In English thus :—" It remains that I remind you of the custom of giving and receiving baptism. The right of giving it belongs to the highest priest, who is the bishop. Then to the presbyters and deacons, yet not without the bishop's authority, *for the sake of the honour of the church* This being secured, peace is secured *Otherwise* even the laity have the right." Does this also "entirely agree" with what Dr. C. alleges from Ignatius, as to what is essential to the very being of a church by divine institution?

It is proper to apprize the reader that Tertullian is not a writer upon whose speculations we should repose implicit confidence, although as to matters of fact and

* Exhortatio ad Castitatem Tertullian was the first of the Latin fathers, about the beginning of the third century.

† De Bap cap. xvii

custom he may be regarded as an ordinarily credible witness. The ill usage he received from the ecclesiastics of Rome is supposed to have contributed to make him a Montanist, and thus, as Dr. Jortin remarks, he lost the title of *saint*. The same author adds, that though learned for his time he was deficient in judgment, and fell into many errors Yet, in citing him, as I have done above, I have only to say, that if he be good authority for our opponents, then surely it cannot be unfair to turn their own artillery against themselves. *Tertullian's* opinion then was that the priesthood itself is not of divine original, since by the gospel law all Christians are priests, and that, consequently, the distinction between the priesthood and laity is of the church's making ·—" *propter ecclesiæ honorem —Alioquin etiam laicis jus est* " So Dr Campbell understood him, and so do I ; and it is submitted to the learned reader whether this be not the obvious drift of Tertullian's argument, and the true meaning of the passage cited by Dr C Does Dr. C. affirm that in this also Tertullian and Irenæus " entirely agree," and does he himself adopt the sentiment ?*

---

* The mantle of charity which that ingenious and learned critic Dr. Jortin casts over the learned African father now under review, with all his defects, may well be commended to the consideration of ecclesiastical controvertists and critics, in moderation of that *odium theologicum* which too often disfigures and disgraces their productions , at the same time that the cause of truth itself is wounded through the intemperate zeal of overheated friends After mentioning Tertullian's losing, that is, failing to receive, the title of *saint*, from the cause above stated,—a title, he adds, which hath been often as wretchedly bestowed as other titles and favours,—he thus continues —

" Charity bids us suppose that he lost not what is infinitely more important Several have thought too hardly concerning him ; never considering, that, with all his abilities, he was deficient in judgment, and had a partial disorder in his understanding, which excuses almost as much as downright phrensy He was learned for those times, acute and ingenious, and somewhat satirical, hasty, credulous, impetuous, rigid and censorious, fanatical and enthusiastical, and a bad writer as to style, not perhaps through incapacity of doing better, but through a false taste and a perverse affectation He fell into many errors but it is to be hoped that in another world the

But if Dr. C means merely, as is possible, that Tertullian and Irenæus entirely agree as to the succession of the early bishops of Rome, then let us examine this point. Turning back to the translation of a translation of the third chapter of Irenæus's third book against heresies, as furnished by Dr. C., pages 71, 72, I find it there stated, as the *tradition* of the Church of Rome, that that church was founded " by the two most glorious apostles Peter and Paul ;" whereas Tertullian, in his account of the tradition of the same church, omits the name of Paul, and says that it " tells of Clement ordained by *Peter* "

Again. Irenæus says, " The blessed apostles [not Peter alone] delivered the bishopric to *Linus* "Tertullian says the tradition was that *Peter* delivered it to *Clement* *

Again. Irenæus says, that it was after both *Linus* and *Anacletus*, that " *in the third place* from the apostles Clement obtained the bishopric "† Whereas Tertullian says he was ordained directly by *Peter* Is this what Dr C asserts to be an entire agreement? It strikes me, on the contrary, as widely differing in every particular.

Now that I am on this point of the *successions* of the bishops of Rome, it may not be amiss to trace it a little farther And here, I am sure, the reader cannot but be more forcibly struck with the inexplicable confusion and the irreconcilable contradiction which reign at the very head of the line , especially when he considers what stress is laid on this thing by the high-church sect, and that after all it is a mere matter of tradition, and of a tradition so ill at agreement even with itself. If such

mistakes as well as the doubts of poor mortals are rectified, and forgiven too, and that whosoever loves truth and virtue,

> ———— illic postquam se lumine vero
> Implevit, stellasque vagas miratus et astra
> Fixa polo, vidit quanta sub nocte jaceret
> Nostra dies "

Remarks on Ecclesias Hist vol 1. p. 353.

* Dr C., page 91   † Page 72.

be the true state of the case with regard to the very fountain spring, what possible certainty can there be in its ramified streams? And is this a foundation for such a superstructure as high church would rear upon it?

At the very outset of an attempt to trace this matter farther, the fact presents itself, not only that Tertullian does not agree with Irenæus, but that he does not agree even with himself "His list," says Dr. C.,* "is as follows. Linus, Cletus, Anacletus, Clemens, Evaristus, &c." Now, but a little before, p 91, Dr. C had himself adduced a passage from a different work of Tertullian's, in which it was stated that the tradition was that Clement was ordained to the bishopric by Peter, whereas in this list he stands in the *fourth* place in the succession Irenæus, as has been shown, assigns him the *third* place Epiphanius, again, differs from Irenæus by making *Cletus* the *second*, instead of Anacletus ; and from Tertullian by omitting *Anacletus* altogether ; and still farther, he differs from them all, by giving two Evaristuses in the line—which Dr C will have it, is merely mentioning Evaristus's name twice. Nay, Dr C. himself, in attempting to harmonize Tertullian's conflicting statements, only makes a bad matter still worse. for he shows that he contradicts the assertion and the cherished tradition of the church in Rome itself. There, on the spot, the church of the Romans asserted that Clement was ordained the first bishop by Peter. "On the contrary, [says Dr C,] he [Tertullian] says expressly, 'Hac cathedra, Petrus qua sederat ipso, locatum maxima Roma Linum, *primum* considere jussit.' ' In this chair, in which Peter himself had sat, he commanded Linus, settled in Great Rome, *first* to sit.'" †

Here is not only confusion itself confounded, but

* Page 97
† Page 99 [There are memoranda here indicating that the author intended to add more.—Ed.]

palpable and irreconcilable contradiction, amidst which, being wholly at a loss which to believe, the only safe alternative seems to be to reject them all, and especially, as it is altogether uncertain, in fact, whether even Peter himself ever was in Rome *

Dr C. indeed has certainly a very fertile imagination; and conjectures (in which he quotes Cave as supporting him) that the difference between Irenæus and Epiphanius consists merely in *misspelling* names,—the one writing Cletus and the other Anacletus, but both intending only one and the same person We prefer, however, to take the history as it stands, without the emendation of either Dr C. or Cave. For as both Irenæus and Epiphanius were men of " erudition," it is to be presumed that they knew how to spell names of such distinction and notoriety, or to copy "a list," which Dr. Cooke takes upon himself to affirm " was kept in each

* The whole of the traditionary statements (for they are nothing better) imputed to Irenæus and other ancient fathers, respecting the foundation of that "greatest, most ancient and universally known church" of Rome, " by the two most glorious apostles Peter and Paul," have very much the air of the fabrications of a later period For it is certain, in the first place, that the church of Rome was not the " most ancient," if " the greatest," and in the second place, that Paul was not its founder, as is manifest from his own epistle to that church The following observations, from Dr Adam Clarke's preface to his notes on that epistle, place this matter in a clear light.—

" *When*, or by *whom* the gospel was first preached at Rome cannot be ascertained Those who assert that St. *Peter* was its founder, can produce no solid reason for the support of their opinion Had this apostle first preached the gospel in that city, it is not likely that such an event would have been unnoticed in the *Acts of the Apostles*, where the labours of St. Peter are particularly detailed with those of St Paul, which indeed form the chief subject of this book Nor is it likely that the author of this epistle should have made no reference to this circumstance, had it been true. Those who say that this church was founded by these two apostles conjointly have still less reason on their side, for it is evident from chap i, 8, &c , that St Paul had *never been at Rome*, previously to his writing this epistle It is most likely that no *apostle* was employed in this important work, and that the gospel was first preached there by some of those persons who were converted at Jerusalem on the day of Pentecost, for we find from Acts ii, 10 that there were then at Jerusalem *strangers of Rome, Jews, and proselytes*, and these, on their return, would naturally declare the wonders they had witnessed, and proclaim that truth by which they themselves had received salvation,"

church ," and that in a matter of such importance they used diligence and care. And if they did not, then their histories are entitled to the less credit

In coming down to the time of *Cyprian*, a favourite authority with high-church writers, I have no hesitation to grant, not only that by that time the polity of the Christian churches generally was "episcopal," in the proper sense of this term, as indeed I believe it always was, but that Cyprian and other Christian writers of that age used a style clearly expressive of three official distinctions in the ministry, whether denominated orders, degrees, or by whatever other name they may be called   I am free to admit, also, that down to that time, about the middle of the third century, the powers and prerogatives of the bishops had been steadily advancing, and those of the presbyters gradually depressed, so that even at that period, the style and state of bishops, as compared with other presbyters, presented an aspect very different from that which had been exhibited either in the apostolical age, or in that which immediately succeeded the death of the last of the inspired college. At that period, moreover, and increasingly so thereafter, there are plain indications that presbyters were not only restricted from the actual performance of what was deemed the peculiarly sacred function of ordination, at least without the bishop's permission, (and in churches episcopally constituted very properly so,) but that it became very unusual for the bishop to grant this permission , and, as Dr. Campbell has well remarked, the transition from *seldom* to *never* is very natural , and just as natural, in our ways of judging, from what is never done to what cannot lawfully be done.

The true question, however, and the only true question, at this stage of the controversy, still remains, and is wholly unaffected by any of the above admissions. It is not whether presbyters actually did ordain at the period in question, either alone or in conjunction with a bishop as his colleague,—but whether it was even then generally judged and admitted that there either is anything essential in the character of the ministry itself, or of universal and perpetual obligation in its divine institution, which makes it unlawful, invalid, and null for presbyters to perform this function in churches which have no bishops in fact, or with the permission or by the direction of the bishop in those which have, and where there are no laws, usages, or order of such churches to the contrary On *this* question there is not wanting testimony in support of our views, even in Cyprian, as much as he was disposed to exalt the episcopal prerogative, and to bring in an unlimited multitude of popes, while he manfully resisted the arrogant assumptions of one, as above shown

Dr Miller, in reference to the sentiments of Cyprian, had said that he not only repeatedly calls the presbyters of Carthage his *colleagues,* but that in writing to them when he was himself in exile, he requests them, during his absence, to perform *his duties* as well as *their own ,* which seems plainly to imply that he considered them inherently capable in his absence, and by his permission or request, to perform whatever was deemed peculiar to the office of the bishop when present, as well as their own ordinary functions.   Dr. C. answers that Cyprian's words are not quoted , and that, supplying the defect from Hooker, what Cyprian exhorted and commanded his presbyters to do was, "to supply his room in doing those things which *the exercise of religion requires* "*

I ask then, whether the following, from Cyprian's fifth epistle, be not the place to which Dr Miller alludes :—
" Quoniam mihi interesse nunc non permittit loci conditio, peto vos pro fide et religione vestra, *fungamini illic et vestris partibus et meis,* ut nihil vel ad disciplinam vel ad diligentiam desit."

* Page 94

Will not Dr. C undertake to affirm that, to supply his (Cyprian's) room " in doing those things which *the exercise of religion requires*," is " an exact translation" of "*fungamini illic et vestris partibus et meis?*" On the contrary, I appeal to every reader in the least acquainted with the Latin tongue, whether it be not an explicit entreaty to them to perform, in the exigence of his necessary absence, the functions peculiar to his office when present, as well as those ordinarily their own ? And had he intended any limitation, and especially if he meant to except the chief function of all—ordination, would he not have said so, or have given some intimation of it ? Instead of this, he gives them but one simple general rule for their guidance, as long as it might be necessary for him to continue absent, and that was to perform the duties of his office as well as their own.   And I submit it, moreover, to the unmystified understanding of every reader, whether, if a vacancy had actually occurred, either in the deaconship or the eldership of that church during Cyprian's absence, (which would have made it the more especially desirable that it should be filled,) the above request would not have been a sufficient warrant, so far as Cyprian's sanction was concerned, to authorize the presbytery to proceed to supply such vacancy by an actual ordination.

This view of the subject is greatly strengthened by the following passage, in a letter to Cyprian from Firmilian bishop of Cæsarea, one of his contemporaries.— " Quando omnis potestas et gratia in ecclesia constituta sit, ubi præsident majores natu, qui et baptizandi et manum imponendi, et ordinandi possident potestatem "* That is, " Since all power and grace is established in the church, where elders preside, who have the power both of baptizing and imposing hands, and *ordaining* " On the original Latin of this passage, as above, the fol-

* Cyprian's Epis., p 75

lowing remarks of Dr Campbell are so clear and satis-
factory that I add them entire

"That by *majores natu*, in Latin, is meant the same
with πρεσβυτεροι in Greek, of which it is indeed a literal
version, can scarcely be thought questionable   Besides,
the phrase so exactly coincides with that of Tertullian, who says, ' Probati præsident seniores,'—approved
elders preside,—as to make the application, if possible,
still clearer.   Indeed, if we were not to consider the
Latin, majores natu, as meant to correspond to the
Greek πρεσβυτεροι, the only translation we could give to the
phrase used by Firmilian would be, 'where old men
preside ,' an affirmation which could hardly ever have
been in such general terms given with truth.   For
when the canonical age of bishops came to be established, it was no more than thirty ; and it is a certain
fact that, both before and after that canon, several were
ordained younger.   I am far from thinking that under
this term, ' majores natu,' those who were then peculiarly called bishops are not included, or even principally intended   but what I maintain is, that, now
that the distinction had obtained, the use of so comprehensive a term seems sufficiently to show that it
was not his intention to affirm it of the latter order,
exclusively of the former, else he would never have
employed a word which, when used strictly, was appropriated to the former order and not to the latter —
Thus the name *priests*, in English, in the plural number, is often adopted to denote the clergy in general,
both bishops and priests   But no intelligent person
that understands the language, and does not intend to
deceive, would express himself in this manner—' In the
Church of England the priests have the power of baptizing, confirming, and ordaining.'   Nor could he excuse
himself by pretending that in regard to the two last articles, he meant by the word priests the bishops, exclusively of those more commonly, and for distinction's

sake, called priests. Yet the two cases are exactly parallel, for in Firmilian's time the distinction of the three orders was, though not so considerable, as well known by the Christians in Cappadocia and in Africa, as they are at this day in England."*

These just and forcible observations are also a full answer to a remark which Dr C makes, p. 96, on Dr. Miller's reference to the above passage, and which is so frequently repeated throughout his book, viz, "that some writers occasionally used the general term presbyter, or priest, in speaking of the bishop" That they sometimes used the general term presbyters, or priests, *inclusively* of the bishop or bishops, is granted But after that the distinction of three orders became general, as was the case in Firmilian's time, no sensible writer would choose this comprehensive term in describing the functions peculiar to bishops, as contradistinguished from, and exclusively of, presbyters, to whom, strictly, this designation is appropriate. On this point Dr Campbell's illustration seems to me perfectly conclusive. "The name *priests*, in English, in the plural number, is often adopted to denote the clergy in general, both bishops and priests. But no intelligent person, that understands the language, and does not intend to deceive, would express himself in this manner—'In the Church of England the priests have the power of baptizing, confirming, and ordaining.' Nor could he excuse himself by pretending that in regard to the last two articles, he meant by the word priests the bishops, exclusively of those more commonly, and for distinction's sake, called priests" In regard to the parallel passage of Tertullian, quoted by Dr. Campbell as illustrative of the *majores natu* of Firmilian, Dr C thinks that the phrase, "Præsident probati quique seniores," means "that certain approved *old men* presided;" and then

* Lectures on Ecclesiastical History, pp. 114, 115

adds, "and this term is so general that it certainly does not indicate presbyters particularly "* If by "particularly," Dr C. means *exclusively*, it is granted. But does this general term *exclude presbyters?* Does it indicate bishops in Dr. C's sense of bishops, and bishops only? This is the true question, and common sense, with common honesty, may answer it

In addition to what Dr Campbell says as to the rendering of the phrase " old men," that it imputes to the writer an affirmation which could hardly ever, in such general terms, have been made with truth,—I may cite a passage from one of the letters of Ignatius, as furnished by Dr C himself " Wherefore it will become you also not to use your bishop too familiarly, *upon the account of his youth ,* not considering his age, which indeed to appearance is *young* " Epist to the Magnesians. So also Paul to Timothy, "Let no man despise thy *youth* "

As to the observation which Dr C somewhere makes, that the period anciently denominated " youth" extended to a considerable age, it is wholly irrelevant; because, in the first place, the writers of those times would not call *old men* those whom their language and custom classed among the young , and in the second, the very charges given both by Ignatius and St Paul show that Timothy and the Magnesian bishop were young in fact, and therefore liable to be treated too familiarly, if their elevated character and conduct did not protect them against it

But of all the extraordinary things in Dr C's book, his representations of the views of *Jerome* surprise me most Whether he has exhibited them justly and truly, the reader shall have an opportunity to judge

I had before occasion to remark, incidentally, that Jerome was a Christian writer of the latter part of the fourth century. "A man," says Dr. Campbell, " who

* Page 88

had more erudition than any other person then in the
church, the greatest linguist, the greatest critic, the
greatest antiquary of them all." This will probably not
be disputed, and consequently the reader may well
suppose that he was capable of expressing himself in-
telligibly on a subject which he professedly took in
hand to treat Now let it be carefully observed, that
the question here, for the present, is not whether Jerome's views were right or wrong, but *what were they,*
and has Dr C correctly and fairly represented them?
In the days of Jerome, then, it seems that some deacon
had taken upon him to assert that the order of deacons
was superior to that of presbyters. To come at his
error, and at the same time to chastise his arrogance,
Jerome, in his epistle to Evagrius, says:—" I hear that
a certain person has broken out into such folly, that he
prefers *deacons* before *presbyters,* that is, before *bishops;*
for when the apostle clearly teaches that *presbyters* and
bishops were the *same,* who can endure it that a *minister
of tables and of widows* should proudly exalt himself
above those at whose prayers the body and blood of
Christ is made? Do you seek for authority? Hear that
testimony,—*Paul and Timothy, servants of Jesus Christ,
to all the saints in Christ Jesus that are at Philippi, with
the bishops and deacons* Would you have another example? In the Acts of the Apostles *Paul* speaks thus
to the priests of one church: *Take heed to yourselves,
and to all the flock over which the Holy Ghost hath made
you bishops, that you govern the church which he hath purchased with his own blood* And lest any one should contend about there being a plurality of bishops in one
church, hear also another testimony, by which it may
most manifestly be proved that a bishop and presbyter
are the same. *For this cause left I thee in Crete, that
thou shouldst set in order the things that are wanting, and
ordain presbyters in every city, as I have appointed thee.
If any be blameless, the husband of one wife, &c For a*

bishop must be blameless as steward of God And to *Timothy, Neglect not the gift that is in thee, which was given thee by prophecy, by the laying on of the hands of the presbytery.* And *Peter*, also, in his first epistle saith, *The presbyters which are among you I exhort, who am also a presbyter, and a witness of the sufferings of Christ, and also a partaker of the glory that shall be revealed, to rule the flock of Christ, and to inspect it, not of constraint, but willingly, according to God,* which is more significantly expressed in the Greek Επισκοπουντες, that is, superintending it, whence the *name* of *bishop* is drawn Do the testimonies of such men seem small to thee ? Let the evangelical trumpet sound, the *son of thunder,* whom Jesus loved much, who drank the streams of doctrine from our Saviour's breast *The presbyter to the elect lady and her children, whom I love in the truth.* And in another epistle, *The presbyter to the beloved Gaius, whom I love in the truth* But that one was *afterward* chosen, who should be set above the rest, was done as a remedy against schism ; lest every one drawing the church of Christ to himself, *should break it in pieces* For at *Alexandria*, from *Mark* the evangelist, to *Heraclas* and *Dionysius*, the bishops thereof, the presbyters always named one, chosen from among them, and placed in a higher degree, *bishop.* As if an army should make an emperor, or the *deacons* should choose one of themselves, whom they knew to be most diligent, and call him *archdeacon* " Miller's Letters, pp. 184, 185

Again. in his commentary on St Paul's epistle to Titus, the same very eminent father says —

"Let us diligently attend to the words of the apostle, saying, *That thou mayest ordain elders in every city, as I have appointed thee* Who, discoursing in what follows what sort of presbyter is to be ordained, saith, *If any one be blameless, the husband of one wife, &c*, afterward adds, *For a bishop must be blameless, as the steward of God, &c* A *presbyter*, therefore, is the *same* as a *bishop,* and before there were, by the devil's instinct, parties in religion, and it was said among the people, *I am of Paul, and I of Apollos, and I of Cephas,* the churches were governed by the common council of presbyters But *afterward,* when every one thought that those whom he baptized were rather his than Christ's, it was determined through the whole world that one of the presbyters should be set above the rest, to whom all care of the church should belong, that the seeds of schism might be taken away If any suppose that it is merely *our* opinion, and not that of the Scriptures, that bishop and presbyter are the same, and that one is the name of *age,* the other of *office,* let him read the words of the apostle to the *Philippians,* saying, *Paul and Timothy, the servants of Jesus Christ, to all the saints in Christ Jesus that are at Philippi; with the bishops and deacons Philippi* is a city of *Macedonia,* and certainly in one city there could not be more than one bishop, as they are *now* styled But at that time they called the same men *bishops* whom they called *presbyters,* therefore he speaks indifferently of bishops as of presbyters This may seem even yet doubtful to some, till it be proved by another testimony. It is written in the Acts of the Apostles, that when the apostle *came to Miletus. he sent to Ephesus, and called the presbyters of that church,* to whom, among other things, he said, *Take heed to yourselves, and to all the flock over whom the Holy Ghost hath made you bishops, to feed the church of God which he hath purchased with his own blood.* Here observe diligently, that calling together the presbyters of one city, *Ephesus,* he afterward styles the same persons *bishops* If any will receive that epistle which is written in the name of *Paul* to the *Hebrews,* there also the care of the church is divided among many, since he writes to the people, *Obey them that have the rule over you, and submit yourselves, for they watch for your souls, as those that must give an account, that they may do it with joy and not with grief, for that is unprofitable for you* And *Peter* (so called from the firmness of his faith) in his epistle saith, *The presbyters which are among you I exhort, who am also a presbyter, and a witness of the sufferings of Christ, and also a partaker of the glory that shall be revealed, Feed the flock of God which is among you, not by constraint, but willingly.* These things I have written to show that among the ancients *presbyters* and *bishops* were the same But, *by little and little,* that all the seeds of dissension might be plucked up, the whole care was devolved on *one.* As, therefore, the *presbyters* know that *by the custom of the church* they are subject to him who is their *president,* so let *bishops* know that they are above *presbyters* more *by the custom of the church* than by the *true dispensation of Christ;* and that they ought to rule the church in common, imitating *Moses,* who, when he might *alone* rule the people of Israel, chose seventy with whom he might judge the people " Miller's Letters, pp 180–183.

After carefully perusing the above passages, without reference to any purposes of party or system, can any intelligent and candid reader doubt that Jerome intended (in vindication of the true primitive order of presbyters as divinely instituted, and in correction of the assuming deacon whose presumption was the occasion of the first passage) to assert,

1 That in the apostolical age, and by the Divine institution, bishops and presbyters were one and the same order and that what he had written then was expressly to show that " among the ancients" this was the case.

2 That it was as a remedy against schisms, after that age, viz · when every one thought that those whom he baptized were rather his than Christ's, that it was determined through the whole world, that one of the presbyters should be set above the rest, to whom subsequently, and fully so by Jerome's time, the title *bishop* came to be distinctively appropriated

6

3 That the above change in the government of the churches took place, not all at once, but *gradually*, (*paulatim*,) *by little and little*. How long it was before it became general or universal not being stated

4 That the true footing of the acquired superiority of bishops above presbyters was, that *by the custom of the church*, rather than by the *true dispensation of Christ*, they had, *by little and little*, been elevated to the *official* superiority of *presidents*, or presiding presbyters, to whom the rest, with their free consent, as seems plainly implied, and for the sake of order and harmony, had become subjected In other words, that this state of things gradually took the place of the original primitive order, and was of the church's making, though for expedient and salutary purposes, and not of Divine institution, or by divine right.

5. That the presidency or official superiority of bishops, which thus gradually took place in the church, was no other than such as the body of presbyters themselves could and did confer. In proof of which, and in evidence that this actual practice had not wholly ceased until a comparatively late period, he adduces the noted instance of the famous church at Alexandria, as above recited.

This summary of Jerome's sentiments, which I beg the reader to compare with the passages above quoted, makes him consistent with himself, and with the express object of his letter to Evagrius, which was to show that presbyters, so far from being inferior to deacons, as some vain deacon had weakly or proudly asserted, were primarily of the same order with *bishops* A contrary interpretation, on the other hand, makes his argument incoherent, inconsistent, and subversive of his avowed design.

Dr. Miller remarks that it might be a matter of surprise to learn that some episcopal writers had ventured to say that Jerome merely *conjectured* that in the apostle s days bishops and presbyters were the same. What surprise may not justly be excited, to learn that *Dr C.* has the controversial hardihood roundly to affirm, and to endeavour to make his readers believe, "that *this passage from Jerome, taken as it is offered,* [that is, as I understand, taken as quoted by Dr. Miller, and above from him,] *plainly declares* that *episcopacy* [of course in the high-church sense asserted by Dr C] was established through the whole world by a decree   in the time of Paul and the other apostles, and consequently *was done by them,* and is therefore a Divine institution." In other words, as he had said a little before, that it was done " by all the apostles; originated with these inspired servants of God, and is therefore a Divine institution, and absolutely binding on all the church." All which, whether directly, or by just and fair inference, Dr. C. asserts he has shown "that this passage from Jerome, taken as it is offered, *plainly declares.*"*

That I do not misunderstand Dr. C. seems entirely clear from the various forms and places in which, in substance, he repeats this assertion, and especially from a sentence toward the conclusion of his discussion of this subject, in which he says,—"It is *evident from the preceding examination of the passages from Jerome, quoted by Dr Miller,* that he [Jerome] *fully supports the doctrine that episcopacy* [of course in Dr. C's sense] *was established by the apostles.*"† On which ground, as the very footing on which Jerome "plainly" places the matter, Dr C had asserted before that it is "therefore a Divine institution, and absolutely binding on all the church!"

As the reader may possibly be curious to know by what occult power of the magical art Dr C., through some twenty large pages, elaborates this extraordinary conclusion, and puts this perfect fool's-cap on Jerome,

* Pages 102, 103.   † Page 117

I will endeavour, if I can, to make an abstract of it,—interspersing, by the way, some occasional observations on the process

The grand fulcrum on which the whole lever of his argument rests, is the observation which Jerome makes in his commentary on Titus, in which, after saying, " a presbyter, therefore, is the same as a bishop,' he adds, " and before there were, by the devil's instinct, parties in religion, and it was said among the people *I am of Paul, I of Apollos, and I of Cephas,* the churches were governed by the common council of presbyters. But *afterward,* when every one thought that those whom he baptized were rather his than Christ's, it was determined through the whole world, that one of the presbyters should be set above the rest, to whom all care of the church should belong, that the seeds of schism might be taken away "

Now, says Dr. C, " the date of the circumstance mentioned by Jerome as having produced the change he speaks of, is easily determined This circumstance is mentioned in Paul's first epistle to the Corinthians, (i, 12)—" He then goes into a detail to show the date of that epistle, and concludes thus " This was therefore done by the apostles themselves, and because done by inspired men, it is a divine institution "* The same thing, grounded on the same assumption, he reiterates over and over, throughout the twenty pages

There are three [four] considerations, however, which totally overthrow this main pillar of Dr. C 's whole argument

1 The first is. as suggested by Dr Miller, that some of the portions of the New Testament from which Jerome adduces proof that bishops and presbyters were originally the same, were certainly written *after* the first epistle to the Corinthians From which it is manifest

* Page 101

that Jerome could not, without palpably contradicting himself, have intended to say that it was just at that time, when that first epistle to the Corinthians was written, that the change took place of which he speaks, and that it was then done by the decree of "all the apostles" themselves, for all the churches "through the whole world"

2 Dr C's arguments involve anachronisms which convict them of palpable error. In a former part of his work he undertook "to show from the Scripture," that it was in the state of anxiety for the welfare of the Ephesian church, in which Paul left Ephesus to go into Macedonia, as related in the twentieth chapter of Acts, that he committed to Timothy the episcopal charge of that church, that his first epistle to Timothy, containing "full evidence of ample episcopal authority,"—that is, of the ample episcopal authority committed to Timothy by Paul,—"was written in *Macedonia*, after Paul went there from Greece, and *before* he rejoined Timothy and the rest of his company at Troas "*

Now if the reader will take the trouble to look at the twentieth chapter of the Acts of the Apostles, he will see indisputable proof that all this was *before* Paul came to *Miletus*, and thence sent for the elders of Ephesus to meet him there. If he will look at page 101 of Dr. C.'s book, he will also find that Paul's placing Timothy over the Ephesian church at that period, is alleged by Dr C. as one of the instances of the change made in pursuance of the apostolical decree, on the occasion mentioned in first Corinthians. And yet it is on Paul's address to the elders of Ephesus at *Miletus, subsequently* to Timothy's being made bishop of Ephesus, according to Dr C , that Jerome founds one of his principal arguments for the primitive identity of bishops and presbyters' Is it possible, then, that *Jerome's* views and *Dr C's* could be the same?

* Pages 32–36.

3 Dr C. alleges also that Paul " set Titus over the Cretans" " in like manner, and with similar [episcopal] powers " that is, as he had set Timothy over the Ephesians. " And other apostles [Dr C. adds] did the same in other places."* And these episcopal appointments of Timothy and Titus by Paul, with others similar by other apostles in other places, he affirms were the very changes to which Jerome alludes, made " by the apostles themselves," at the time mentioned in first Corinthians i, 12, and yet it was on Paul's epistle to Titus *after* he was placed in Crete, that Jerome founds his argument that bishops and presbyters were the same in the apostolical institutions and language at the time when that epistle was written !

4 The last consideration I shall mention is, that Dr C 's interpretation puts on Jerome a perfect fool's-cap Because his express object was to show that as *presbyters* know that it is *by the custom of the church* that they are subject to him who is their *president*, so *bishops* ought to know that they are above presbyters, more *by the custom of the church* than *by the true dispensation of Christ* The very reverse of which Dr. C.'s construction forces upon him

The only rational construction, therefore, which it would seem, in fairness to Jerome, can be put upon his language is, that his reference to the passage in first Corinthians is by way of *allusion* merely, in the same manner as we still describe such parties in churches as addict themselves to favourite ministerial leaders, by representing them as saying, ' I am of Paul, and I of Apollos, and I of Cephas."

There was one consequence which Dr C found his construction involved in, which, one would think, should have convinced him that he had misinterpreted Jerome. This distinguished father expressly says, that before

* Page 101.

there were by the devil's instinct such parties in religion as he speaks of, "the churches were governed by the common council of presbyters" No, says Dr. C., "he is certainly wrong in saying that, even before the divisions at Corinth the church was governed by a common council of presbyters, except in subordination to the authority of the apostles "* Certainly, Dr C , if Jerome had said so it would have been "certainly wrong," and he certainly was sufficiently acquainted with the New Testament to know this, and would never have risked his reputation on so silly an assertion. But he never said so, and the manifest absurdity of it proves that he never meant so, but that his allusion was to a period subsequent to the apostolical age, when the churches no longer enjoyed the superintendence of inspired guides and rulers; and when *ministers* also—not the *people* merely, as in Corinth—began to form parties for themselves rather than to make disciples of Christ Dr C. might, therefore, have well spared himself the long chain of argumentation by which he *gravely* labours to disprove the imputed sentiment of Jerome. The passages quoted from that very learned father do not express it, and there is the amplest reason to believe that he never entertained it

But Dr. C thinks that he finds a flaw in Dr. Miller's *translation* of *one word* in the quotations from Jerome, which he conceives calculated to support the idea "that a long time elapsed before bishops were set over the churches" The word objected to in the translation is "*afterward.*" That this word necessarily implies "a long time" after, I cannot perceive However, Dr. C. states that the word used by Jerome, according to Jeremy Taylor, is *postquam,* on which he then takes the occasion to furnish a critical disquisition of considerable length to prove that *postquam* does not mean *afterward,*

* Page 117.

but *after that,* literally, *after which,* referring to the time when a thing was done, " as [he continues] in this very case from Jerome." That is to say, Dr. C. here affirms that according to the true critical import of this word *postquam,* Jerome meant to be understood that " *before* that time [viz, that precise period spoken of by Paul in his first epistle to the Corinthians] the common council of presbyters governed the church; *after* that, the bishops "* And yet it has been shown above that it was specially to apostolical epistles written *after* that time that Jerome refers, in proof that presbyters and bishops were still the same

But says Dr C, "*postea* is the word Jerome would have used if he had meant what Dr Miller attributes to him "† Well, although I have not Jerome's original work at hand to examine, as it seems neither had Dr. C, yet, as he takes his extract from Jeremy Taylor, I will take mine from Dr Campbell Now Dr Campbell extracts a passage from Jerome, which, if not taken from the same place as that quoted by Taylor, was evidently written by Jerome in reference to precisely the same subject and occasion In that passage, according to Dr Campbell's extract, *postea* is the word used by Jerome, and consequently, by Dr C.'s own admission, means " what Dr Miller attributes to him " The whole sentence, as quoted by Dr Campbell, stands thus — " Quod autem *postea* [Jerome had been speaking immediately before, says Dr. Campbell, of the times of the apostles] unus electus est, qui cæteris præponeretur, in schismatis remedium factum est, ne unusquisque ad se trahens, Christi ecclesiam rumperet."‡

* Page 115   † Ibid

‡ Lect on Eccl Hist. p. 118. [" But that one was *afterward* elected to be set over the rest was for the prevention of schism, that individuals might not sever the church of Christ by drawing off parties to themselves " The distinction between *postquam* and *postea* is too obvious to justify Dr. C 's paride of learning in his very unnecessary attack on Dr Miller's translation. *Postquam* is a conjunction, *postea* an adverb They may both

By Dr. C.'s own concession, then, this point is settled beyond farther controversy In another part of the process under review, Dr. C. asserts that " *the express statement of Jerome*, in the passage quoted by Dr. Miller, [as above given] establishes" the following particulars.— " 1 That the *bishops* of the primitive church were a *distinct order* of clergy from those *presbyters* who were authorized to preach and administer sacraments, and superior to them" 2 "That each bishop had under him a number of congregations, with their pastors, whom he governed" 3 "That this kind of episcopacy was considered by *the whole* primitive church as an institution of Jesus Christ."† (Dr. C.'s numbering of the above particulars is 1, 3, and 5)

Now the reader will please observe, that the question here for the present is not whether this was the actual state of things in the primitive church,—that is, in the apostolical age, as is obviously meant,—but whether, in the passage quoted from Jerome by Dr. Miller, and copied above, it is " *the express statement of Jerome*," that it was so, and was so considered " by *the whole* primitive church " This is Dr. C.'s unqualified asseveration. But although I have read over the passage in question again and again, and as carefully as I am able, if any one can find in it any such " express statement of Jerome" as Dr. C. avers it to contain, I must confess that his ocular as well as his mental vision must be strangely different from mine

Assuming then that the first and second of the above particulars (Dr. C.'s first and third) are established " by the express statement of Jerome," his next step in the process is to affirm that another " flows from them," viz , " that these bishops were exclusively invested with

mean *after that*, but in different senses, as the English reader will perceive by an example —" *After that* [*postquam*] presbyters ceased to rule the church, bishops governed it " " Presbyters first governed the church, *after that*, [*postea*,] bishops "—Ed]
      † Page 104

the right of ordaining." To this the answer simply is, that Jerome's express statement establishes no such thing as Dr. C affirms it does in the second particular above mentioned; and consequently, that this farther one said to "flow from" the others is equally imaginary Its foundation being taken away it falls itself, of course

In confirmation of his inference, however, Dr C repeats a passage quoted by Dr. Bowden from Jerome, as follows. "For what does a bishop which a presbyter may not do, excepting ordination" And then adds,—"This passage shows plainly that the presbyters had not the power of ordaining, but that this belonged exclusively to the bishop"* It shows plainly that this was the case in Jerome's time, about the close of the fourth century, I grant, but it shows nothing more. Indeed the whole drift of his argument, and the language he uses, both demonstrate that this was what he meant. He had been expressly proving that no distinction originally existed between bishops and presbyters; that they were one and the same order; and that in the church of Alexandria, even down to a comparatively late period, presbyters had constituted their own bishop whenever a vacancy occurred, as the army in the days of imperial Rome made an emperor, or the deacons formerly an archdeacon.† He then comes down to his own

---

* Page 107.

† With this case before him is it not surprising that Dr. C should make the assertion he does, pp 140, 141, that up [down¹] to the time of Eusebius in the fourth century, there is no case of ordination by presbyters, as he believes, "even alleged" by the opponents of the high-church scheme¹ In contradiction of this, I need only cite that very eminent critic, Dr Campbell, whose works are common in this country as well as in Europe, who, in reference to this very case, thus expresses himself —"I know it has been said that this relates only to the election of the bishop of Alexandria, and not to his ordination To me it is manifest that it relates to both, or, to express myself with greater precision, it was the intention of that father [Jerome] to signify that no other ordination than this election, and those ceremonies with which the presbyters might please to accompany it, such as the installment and salutation, was then and there thought necessary to

time, using the *present tense* of the verb, not the past,—
" Quid enim *facit*, excepta ordinatione, episcopus, quod
presbyter not *faciat* " " What *does* a bishop ? " &c As
if he had said, " Even now, what power does a bishop
exercise which a presbyter may not exercise, except the

one who had been ordained a presbyter before , that, according to the
usage of that church, this form was all that was requisite to constitute one
of the presbyters their bishop " Lect on Eccles Hist , p 117. Here
then is alleged *a series of instances*, before the time of Eusebius, in one of
the most renowned churches of antiquity, of the ordination in form or in
fact even of *bishops* by *presbyters* Yet Dr C , with his characteristic
boldness of assertion, affirms in another place, page 116, that " before the
fourth century such a thing [as ordination by presbyters] does not appear to
have been thought of '"

But long before Dr Campbell the same thing was alleged, in terms, if
possible, still more explicit, by that most reverend, very learned primate of
Ireland, *Archbishop Usher* In his letter to Dr Bernard, that eminent
Episcopalian says,—" I have ever declared my opinion to be that *episcopus
et presbyter, gradu tantum different non ordine*, [that *bishop* and *presbyter*
differ in *degree* only, not in *order*,] and consequently, that in places where
bishops cannot be had, the ordination by presbyters stands valid " And in
his answer to Baxter the same distinguished prelate says, " that the king
[Charles I] having asked him at the Isle of Wight, whether he found in
antiquity that *presbyters alone ordained any* ? he replied Yes, and that he
could show his majesty more,—*even where presbyters alone successively
ordained bishops* and instanced in Hierom's [Jerome's] words, (*Epist. ad
Evagrium*) of the presbyters of Alexandria *choosing* and *making* their own
bishops, from the days of Mark till Heraclas and Dionysius " This then
was alleged by that very learned episcopal antiquary, not only as a case of
ordination by presbyters before the time of Eusebius, but of the *successive
ordinations of bishops* by presbyters for about two hundred years It shows,
moreover, that *he* understood Jerome exactly in the sense here averred
And it ought not to be forgotten, that, in addition to his pre-eminent qualifications as a critic and antiquary, he was himself an *archbishop* *

The *Smectymnian* divines, in the same age with Usher, alleged various
proofs of presbyters ordaining, evidently within the period alluded to by
Dr C † *Smectymnuus* was a fictitious name composed of the initial letters
of the names of *Stephen Marshal, Edward Calamy, Thomas Young,
Matthew Newcomen*, and *William Spurstow*

The Rev Ezekiel Cooper, an eminent and venerable minister of the Methodist Episcopal Church, alleged the same in his Funeral Discourse on the
late Bishop Asbury ‡ It was also alleged in the work entitled " A Defence
of our Fathers, and of the original Organization of the Methodist Episcopal
Church "

* Dr C takes upon him to say p 180, that there is no author produced in support of
the latter statement, above mentioned, in reference to Archbishop Usher, and yet, in the
note to Neal's History of the Puritans, the authority for it is distinctly stated Neal's
History of the Puritans, Am Ed vol ii, pp 412, 413, note, and the reference there to
Baxter's Life, p 206
† Ibid p 412
‡ Appendix, pp 218, 219

single one of ordaining?" And even this superiority, in the single item of ordaining, according to the tenor of Jerome's whole argument, was "*by the custom of the church*," (*consuetudine ecclesiæ*,) rather than by "*the true dispensation of Christ*." that is, of the Church's making, and not of Divine institution. It may not be amiss to observe, that even among the papal doctors and theologues in the famous council of Trent, the sentiment last named was precisely the construction put on the language of Jerome ; and it was added that St Austin, (Augustine,) another very eminent father of that age, and himself a very distinguished bishop, was of the same opinion Some disputed in the council that "the degree of a bishop was an *order ,* and others that aboue priesthood there was nothing but *iurisdiction*—and some beeing of a middle opinion, that is, that it is an *eminent dignitie,* or *office* in the *order* The famous saying of St. *Hierom,* [Jerome,] and the authority of St *Austin,* [Augustine] were alleaged, who say that the degree of a bishop hath been most ancient, but yet an ecclesiasticall constitution "*

But what is yet most amazing, if any thing in Dr C. can any longer amaze, after himself quoting a plain explicit passage in Jerome in proof that a presbyter could do every thing that a bishop did, with *one single exception,*—that of ordination,—in the very next paragraph he says, "It is shown by another passage from Jerome, 'that there was also *another* thing that a bishop did which a presbyter could not do, viz., *confirmation* · thus in the same breath making Jerome affirm and deny the same proposition. Is it not more probable that Dr C. misinterprets Jerome in the place last alluded to, and from which he draws his inference, (for it is but an inference,) than that that eminent father thus palpably contradicts himself? One would suppose that the obscure passage should rather be interpreted by the plain one.

* Paul Sarpis' Hist of the Coun of Trent, p 591

Another conclusion at which Dr. C arrives, in the logical process under review, is, that "in Jerome's estimation *apostles and bishops were the same*"*

Now it has been most unequivocally proved above, that "in Jerome's estimation," in the apostles' days, *bishops* and *presbyters* were the same: and as things equal to one and the same thing must necessarily be equal to each other, it follows most conclusively that "in Jerome's estimation" *apostles* and *presbyters* were the same If Dr C rejects this consequence, I still submit it to the reader.

All that Dr. C. says in regard to the Alexandrian ordinations by presbyters,—even of bishops by presbyters,—will be so completely, and I must think conclusively answered in an extract on that subject from an eminent critic, which I shall presently submit to the reader, that I judge it preferable to waive any remarks of my own in regard to it, when others so vastly better than any I am capable of are furnished to my hand

I may just observe, by the way, that I have become so familiarized in Dr C's style with such phrases as the following—"it is impossible that they could have been ordained by presbyters,"—"neither can it be believed,"—"could not possibly have passed unnoticed," &c, &c, that they no longer occasion me any alarm. And it has particularly occurred to me that, *possibly*, there may be a wider range in *possibility* than Dr C. has well considered

He adds as a final remark, too, that " Blondel admits that episcopacy was established in Alexandria above a century before this."† We admit more, viz, that it was episcopal all the while,—its *bishops* being both chosen and ordained, in fact if not in form, by its presbyters, as shall presently be more fully shown

But says Dr C, "It must not be forgotten that Dr.

Miller in this attempt to prove that the second ordination was performed by presbyters, has been driven *to admit a second ordination*"—" a second ordination to what?" he exclaims His own reply is, "To a superior order, necessarily Certainly [he continues] not to an inferior station,—surely not to the same he then occupied, necessarily, therefore, to a superior"* Now mark : Dr C 's assertion here is, that such a second ordination by *presbyters*, as Dr. Miller had contended was the practice in the Alexandrian church, supposing it to have actually taken place, *necessarily constituted a superior order* Be it so , for we will not dispute about the *word* " order " Whether it be called order, degree, or office, it matters not to us the *thing* is what we look at and Dr C. has here furnished us, out of his own mouth, a complete answer to the main objection which has ever been urged by Dr C and his party against the episcopacy of the Methodist Episcopal Church, which rests precisely on this basis I wish to add nothing to what Dr. C concedes in this passage for the complete vindication of our episcopal organization, except, in the words of Jerome, that it is *by the custom of the church,—an ecclesiastical constitution,*—and not pretended to be by *divine right*, nor of essential or universal obligation

The extract that I promised above in support of the views I have taken of the ordinations in the apostolical church of Alexandria for two hundred years or more, and of the true testimony of Jerome, in farther answer to Dr C.'s remarks on these subjects, I now subjoin. It is from the pen of Dr. Campbell

"The testimony which I shall bring from him [Jerome, says this able critic] regards the practice that had long subsisted at Alexandria I shall give you the passage in his own words, from his epistle to Evagrius 'Alexandriæ a Marco evangelista usque ad Heraclam et Dio-

* Page 112

nysium episcopos, presbyteri semper unum ex se electum, in excelsiori gradu collocatum, episcopum nominabant. quomodo si exercitus imperatorem faciat aut diaconi eligant de se quem industrium noverint, et archidiaconum vocent' I know it has been said that this relates only to the election of the bishop of Alexandria, and not to his ordination To me it is manifest that it relates to both ; or, to express myself with greater precision, it was the intention of that father to signify that no other ordination than this election,—and those ceremonies with which the presbyters might please to accompany it, such as the instalment and salutation, —was then and there thought necessary to one who had been ordained a presbyter before , that according to the usage of that church this form was all that was requisite to constitute one of the presbyters their bishop But as I am sensible that unsupported assertions are entitled to no regard on either side, I shall assign my reasons from the author's own words, and then leave every one to judge for himself. Jerome, in the preceding part of this letter, had been maintaining in opposition to some deacon who had foolishly boasted of the order of deacons as being superior to the order of presbyters,—Jerome, I say, had been maintaining that in the original and apostolical constitution of the church, bishop and presbyter were but two names for the same office. That ye may be satisfied that what he says implies no less, I shall give it you in his own words— 'Audio quendam in tantam erupisse vecordiam, ut diaconos presbyteris, id est episcopis, anteferret Nam cum apostolus perspicue doceat eosdem esse presbyteros quos episcopos, quid patitur mensarum et viduarum minister, ut supra eos se tumidus efferat.' For this purpose he had in a cursory manner pointed out some of those arguments from the New Testament which I took occasion in a former discourse to illustrate In regard to the introduction of the episcopal order as then commonly

understood, in contradistinction to that of presbyter, he
signifies that it did not exist from the beginning, but
was merely an expedient devised after the times of the
apostles, in order the more effectually to preserve unity
in every church, as in case of differences among the
pastors it would be of importance to have one acknowledged superior in whose determination they were bound
to acquiesce.   His words are, 'Quod autem *postea*,'—
he had been speaking immediately before of the times
of the apostles,—' unus electus est, qui cæteris præponeretur, in schismatis remedium factum est, ne unus
quisque ad se trahens, Christi ecclesiam rumperet.'
Then follows the passage quoted above concerning the
church of Alexandria.   Nothing can be plainer than
that he is giving an account of the first introduction of
the episcopate, (as the word was then understood,) which
he had been maintaining was not a different order from
that of presbyter, but merely a certain pre-eminence
conferred by election for the expedient purpose of preventing schism.   And in confirmation of what he had
advanced that this election was all that at first was re
quisite, he tells the story of the manner that had long
been practised and held sufficient for constituting a
bishop in the metropolis of Egypt   It is accordingly
introduced thus, ' Nam et Alexandriæ,' as a case entirely apposite . to wit, an instance of a church in which
a simple election had continued to be accounted sufficient for a longer time than in other churches,—an
instance which had remained a vestige and evidence of
the once universal practice.   Now if he meant only to
tell us, as some would have it, that there the election of
the bishop was in the presbyters, there was no occasion
to recur to Alexandria for an example, or to a former
period; as that continued still to be a very common, if
not the general practice throughout the church   And
though it be allowed to have been still the custom in
most places to get also the concurrence or consent of

the people, this shows more strongly how frivolous the argument from their being electors would have been in favour of presbyters as equal in point of order to bishops, and consequently superior to deacons; since in regard to most places as much as this could be said concerning those who are inferior to deacons,—the very meanest of the people, who had all a suffrage in the election of their bishop But, understood in the way I have explained it, the argument has both sense and strength in it, and is in effect as follows.—There can be no essential difference between the order of bishop and that of presbyter, since to make a bishop nothing more was necessary at first (and of this practice the church of Alexandria remained long an example) than the nomination of his fellow-presbyters; and no ceremony of consecration was required but what was performed by them, and consisted chiefly in placing him in a higher seat and saluting him bishop

"Add to this, that the very examples this father makes use of for illustration, show manifestly that his meaning must have been as I have represented it His first instance is the election of an emperor by the army, which he calls expressly making an emperor And is it not a matter of public notoriety that the emperors raised in this manner did, from that moment, without waiting any other inauguration, assume the imperial titles and exercise the imperial power? And did they not treat all as rebels who opposed them? If possible, the other example is still more decisive To constitute an archdeacon, in the sense in which the word was then used, no other form of investiture was necessary but his election, which was in Jerome's time solely in his fellow-deacons; though this also, with many other things, came afterward into the hands of the bishop By this example, he also very plainly acquaints us, that the bishop originally stood in the same relation to the presbyters, in which the archdeacon, in his own time, did to the other

7

deacons : and was, by consequence, no other than what the archpresbyter came to be afterward, the first among the presbyters But does not Jerome, after all, admit in the very next sentence the superiority of bishops in the exclusive privilege of ordaining? True: he admits it as a distinction that then actually obtained; but the whole preceding part of his letter was written to evince that from the beginning it was not so. From ancient times he descends to times then modern, and from distant countries he comes to his own, concluding that still there was but one article of moment whereby their powers were discriminated. 'Quid enim facit, excepta ordinatione, episcopus, quod presbyter non faciat?'— This indeed proves sufficiently that at that time presbyters were not allowed to ordain But it can prove nothing more; for in regard to his sentiments about the rise of this difference, it was impossible to be more explicit than he had been through the whole epistle I shall only add, that for my part I cannot conceive another interpretation that can give either weight to his argument or consistency to his words. The interpretation I have given does both, and that without any violence to the expression I might plead Jerome's opinion in this case—I do plead only his testimony. I say I might plead his opinion as the opinion of one who lived in an age when the investigation of the origin of any ecclesiastical order or custom must have been incomparably easier than it can be to us at this distance of time I might plead his opinion as the opinion of a man who had more erudition than any person then in the church—the greatest linguist, the greatest critic, the greatest antiquary of them all But I am no friend to an implicit deference to human authority in matters of opinion Let his sentiments be no farther regarded than the reasons by which they are supported are found to be good I do plead only his testimony, as a testimony in relation to a matter of fact both recent and noto-

7*

rious , since it regarded the then late uniform practice
of the church of Alexandria,—a city which, before
Constantinople became the seat of empire, was, next to
Rome, the most eminent in the Christian world.

"To the same purpose the testimony of the Alexandrian patriarch Eutychius has been pleaded, who, in
his annals of that church, takes notice of the same practice, but with greater particularity of circumstances than
had been done by Jerome   Eutychius tells us that the
number of presbyters therein was always twelve , and
that on occasion of a vacancy in the episcopal chair, they
chose one of themselves, whom the remaining eleven
ordained bishop by imposition of hands and benediction.
In these points it is evident there is nothing that can
be said to contradict the testimony of Jerome   All that
can be affirmed is, that the one mentions particulars
about which the other had been silent.   But it will be
said, there is one circumstance,—the duration assigned
to this custom,—wherein there seems to be a real contradiction   Jerome brings it no farther down than
Heracla and Dionysius, whereas Eutychius represents
it as continuing to the time of Alexander, about fifty
years later.   Now it is not impossible that a circum-
stantiated custom might have been in part abolished at
one time, and in part at another.   But admit that in this
point the two testimonies are contradictory, that will by
no means invalidate their credibility as to those points
on which they are agreed   The difference, on the contrary—as it is an evidence that the last did not copy
from the first, and that they are therefore two witnesses,
and not one—serves rather as a confirmation of the truth
of those articles wherein they concur   And this is our
ordinary method of judging in all matters depending on
human testimony.   That Jerome, who probably spoke
from memory, though certain as to the main point, might
be somewhat doubtful as to the precise time of the abo-
lition of the custom, is rendered even probable by his

mentioning, with a view to mark the expiration of the practice, two successive bishops rather than one. For if he had known certainly that it ended with Heracla, there would have been no occasion to mention Dionysius, and if he had been assured of its continuance to the time of Dionysius, there would have been no propriety in mentioning Heracla."* But says Dr C, "What the ancient church thought of ordination by presbyters may be gathered from the following statements In the fourth century"—dear sir, be pleased to stop; if by "the ancient church" you mean the church in the fourth century, when Constantine, "that truly most excellent and admirable emperor," as, after Wolfgang, you are pleased to call him, had poured in upon the ecclesiastics a flood of wealth and dignities, and the whole hierarchal corps of patriarchs, exarchs, metropolitans, archbishops, bishops, country bishops, archpriests, priests, archdeacons, deacons, acolyths, exorcists, and doorkeepers became organized. Indeed the foundations of the supremacy of the prince of hierarchs, the pope himself, had become in that age pretty securely established, not indeed by the characteristics which should distinguish a Christian bishop, but by the dazzling magnificence and splendour of his see, which *in that century* had become an object of such ambition as to be the occasion of the most barbarous and furious civil war between the contending factions of the rival candidates for the episcopal throne Apostolical mother of churches!—"the greatest, most ancient, and universally known,"—with which "*on account of thy greater pre-eminence,* it is necessary that every church should agree!" This was thy character *in the fourth century,* and spread the baleful influence of thy conspicuous example throughout Christendom; and yet it is from acts of the church in that age as "the ancient church"

* Lect. on Ecclesiastical History, pp. 117–121.

that Dr C brings authorities to settle the question between the rights of presbyters and bishops!—an age in which there were not wanting bishops so insufferably inflated with the arrogant conceit of their lofty pre-eminence, as scarcely to deign to see mortals, or speak to their fellow-servants!

But says Dr C , " The councils of ' the ancient church' in the fourth century, condemned ordinations by presbyters as null, because not performed by them who were bishops verily and indeed "* And how were those councils composed? Dr C. tells us himself, page 140, " The *presbyters* had no seat in councils as principals, but might sit *as representatives of their bishop ;*" that is, when the bishop himself could not be present; as in the case alleged of the bishop of Rome, who, " being unable through age to attend the Council of Nice, was represented by his presbyters."† So that it was by one of the very parties in the question exclusively,—the prelates themselves who composed the councils in those days, by the favour of the emperors who convened them, —that the decisions were made against the presbyters, who were denied a seat except in some instances, as representatives of absent bishops, and of course as subject to their instructions   Were these councils of the *apostolical* pattern? or are the rights of presbyters to be absolutely concluded by *their ex parte* sentence? Yet the very council whose sentence Dr C. alleges as decisive authority in this question,—the Council of Constantinople,—was exclusively thus composed of *one of the parties in the controversy!*

Nay, Dr. C descends even to the councils of the *fifth* century, and alleges the authority of their decrees to the same effect ‡—a century, early in which (as a specimen of the manner in which things were carried *even*

* Page 146.   † Ibid.   ‡ Ibid.

in general councils, in those degenerate days of episcopal arrogance and domination) the lawless, haughty, and imperious Bishop Cyril presided in an œcumenical council, the transactions of which are branded by the learned Mosheim " as full of low artifice, contrary to all the rules of justice, and even destitute of the least air of common decency "* And that this was not a mere exception, a singular instance of unbridled lawlessness and violence in the episcopal councils of that age, appears on the authority of the same eminent historian ; who states, that in another general council, held before the middle of that century, in which Bishop Dioscorus, the successor of Cyril, and the faithful imitator of his arrogance and fury, presided, matters were carried on with the same want of equity and decency that had dishonoured and characterized the proceedings of the one just above named, under the presidency of his predecessor   And if the reader can credit it on the authority of the best historians, such was the infamous brutality of this fifth century council, that even a bishop against whom the lordly and dominant Dioscorus had a pique, was *publicly scourged in the most barbarous manner,* BY THE ORDER OF THE COUNCIL, and died soon after of the bruises inflicted on him in that assembly of *jure divino* [by divine right] *successors of the apostles !*

After such a relation it can be no matter of wonder that a synod in which such atrocities were perpetrated, came afterward to be denominated " συνοδον ληστρικον," a *synod of robbers,* " to signify that every thing was carried in it by fraud or violence "†

I recite such outrages with no pleasure, but with mortification and grief for the Christian name. But since Dr C. thinks it of importance to his cause to urge the ex parte decisions of synods and councils in that age, it is proper that readers who may not be in the

* Vol. ii, p 66   † Ibid. p 74.

habit of looking into such things should be made acquainted with the characters by whom, and the manner in which their transactions were too often governed, as may be well supposed in controversies involving conflicting claims of ecclesiastical prerogative. As regards the particular case of the presbyter *Aerius*, who, on the authority of Epiphanius, is stated by Dr C , p 146, to have been "condemned as a heretic," in the fourth century, because he "maintained that presbyters were equal to bishops, and had a right to ordain ," together with "some other doctrines," as Dr C. adds,—as to his "other doctrines," if they were no worse than that charged in the first count of the indictment against him, above stated, the reader can well imagine what must have been the temper of the assembly that condemned him as a *heretic* for *that cause* He is said, however, to have been a semi-arian , and in so far as this part of the charges against him is concerned, if it be true, we are certainly no more disposed to defend him than Dr. C. But it may not be amiss for the reader to be reminded that denunciations of "heresy," and the mad-dog brand of "heretic" in the age under review and those succeeding it, ought to be received with great caution The Methodist reader especially, whether Arminian or Calvinistic, will be sensible of the appositeness of this admonition, when, if he look into the chronological tables appended to the valuable Ecclesiastical History of Mosheim by the learned translator, he will find under the head of "Heretics, or enemies of revelation," in juxtaposition with the names of the chief infidels of the eighteenth century, the venerated names of "the Moravian brethren, and the followers of Whitefield, Wesley, and others of the same stamp !'" Would to God the world were full of "heretics" of that "same stamp "

One of the leading tenets of Aerius in truth was, "that bishops were not distinguished from presbyters *by any divine right;* but that, according to the institution of the New Testament, their offices and authority were absolutely the same "*   It is perfectly certain, also, as Mosheim adds, that this opinion of his " was highly agreeable to many good Christians, who were no longer able to bear the tyranny and arrogance of the bishops of this century"†—that is, the *fourth* century.

He farther condemned *prayers for the dead*, with some of the stated fasts and festivals, "and other rites of that nature, in which [as Mosheim remarks] the multitude erroneously imagine that the life and soul of religion consists.   His *great purpose* [continues the same historian] seems to have been *that of reducing Christianity to its primitive simplicity,*" is it then any longer to be wondered at, that in those days he should have been condemned as a "heretic" by the courtly prelates who basked in the beams of imperial favour?   And yet, on the whole, his *doctrinal* error alone excepted, intelligent Christians at this day must think very much better of him than of many of those who condemned him.

It ought not to be overlooked also that the work of Bp Epiphanius against heresies, to which Dr. C. refers for authority against Aerius, is characterized by ecclesiastical critics as a work that "has little or no reputation, is full of inaccuracies and errors, and discovers almost in every page the levity and ignorance of its author "‡

But it is time to make the reader acquainted with the truth of the case in regard to Aerius   This I will do in the language of that distinguished Christian antiquary Dr. (afterward Bishop) Stillingfleet

"In the matter itself, [says Stillingfleet,] I believe, upon the strictest inquiry, Medina's judgment will prove

---

*Mosheim, vol 1, p 376   † Ibid.

‡ Mosheim, vol. 1, p 349   Dr Jortin says of Epiphanius that he must have been either a dupe or a deceiver, and that this is the *civilest* thing we can say of him   That " learned and judicious men, who have examined his writings, have been forced to conclude that, with all his learning and piety, [?] he was credulous, careless, censorious, and *one who made no scruple of romancing and misrepresenting* " Remarks on Ecc. Hist , vol 1, pp 301, 302.

true, that Jerome, Austin, Ambrose, Sedulius, Primasius, Chrysostom, Theodoret, Theophylact, were all of Aerius his judgment as to the identity of both name and order of bishops and presbyters in the primitive church; but here lay the difference   Aerius from hence proceeded to separation from bishops and their churches, because they were bishops   And Blondell well observes, that the main ground why Aerius was condemned was for unnecessary separation from the church of Sebastia, and those bishops, too, who agreed with him in other things : whereas, Jerome was so far from thinking it necessary to cause a schism in the church by separating from bishops, that his opinion is clear, that the first institution of them was for preventing schisms; and therefore, for peace and unity, he thought their institution very useful in the church of God "*

Thus it appears that in the judgment of this very deeply versed and able critic in ecclesiastical antiquities, and "upon the strictest inquiry," Aerius, if a heretic in regard to the point now in hand—the identity of the order of bishops and presbyters in the primitive church —was such in very orthodox company, and even that of the canonized *fathers* and *saints*

There is moreover one bearing of the very cases which Dr C. adduces, to which he seems not to have adverted He himself shows sufficiently, that presbyters previously to the prohibitions of the councils alluded to *did ordain*, and did claim the Scriptural *right* to do so, in virtue of their order.   Why else were the ecclesiastical canons made against this practice ?   Why else were such ordinations declared null, *because performed by presbyters ?* The very prohibitions themselves, (as well observed by Dr. Campbell,) the very assertions of those whom they condemned as heretics, prove the practice then probably wearing, but not quite worn out   There was no

* Irenicum, pp 276, 277.

occasion for making canons against ordinations by deacons or by laymen, who did not pretend to such a right.   In deference, however, to the Apostle Paul's authority, perhaps the bishop still admitted, and even required the presbyters present to join with him in ordaining a presbyter by the imposition of their hands with his, but not in ordaining a bishop

As to the case of the founder of the Novatian sect, to which Dr C repeatedly refers, it should be understood that the whole relation of it, as contained in the sixty-third chapter of the sixth book of Eusebius, is made up of the statements of Cornelius, the successful rival and bitter enemy of Novatus, as his own coarse epithets and vulgar abuse plainly show   The usurped domination and impious ignorance of Cornelius are manifest in those same letters of his own, from which Eusebius makes his extracts.   He coolly says, for instance :—" In the roomes of the other bishops [that is, of those who had ordained Novatus] we ordained and sent from us such as should succeed them "   Not forsooth, as is plain enough, because they were " simple countrymen," as he represents, nor even because they were " somewhat tipsie" withal, " and well crammed with victuals," as he also alleges,—but *because they had ordained Novatus*

Again, in the course of the torrent of invectives which he pours out against this late unsuccessful rival in the contest for the episcopal throne in that imperial city, he suggests a doubt, among other things, whether he had ever been canonically baptized, and that afterward, at any rate, he had not obtained confirmation by the hands of the bishop, on which he gravely asks this question,—" Insomuch then as he obtained not that, how came he by the Holy Ghost ?"

Mosheim, on the other hand, founds his relation of the matter on the authority both of Cornelius in Eusebius, and of Cyprian, bishop of Carthage.   For Mosheim represents that the Roman presbyter was named *Nova-tian*, who was assisted in his enterprise by *Novatus*, a presbyter of Carthage, who had come to Rome to escape the resentment of Cyprian, with whom he was highly at variance. So that in reality all the account we have of the matter is from the bitter enemies if not the persecutors of these two presbyters ; and consider-ing human nature, and the evidence which, alas ! our own times afford, that men as good, perhaps, as some even of the Roman or Carthaginian *saints*, too often fol-low its unrestrained and unhallowed impulses in such circumstances, we ought perhaps to receive such state-ments with not a few or inconsiderable grains of al-lowance

With these preliminary observations, I am now prepared to say,—(1.) that having carefully examined the statements of Cornelius in Eusebius, I am well persuaded that they carry on the face of them conclu-sive evidence that they are the vindictive colourings of a personal enemy, and therefore not to be adopted in gross now without large deductions . and (2,) that Novatus doubtless desired episcopal ordination , and may have even too anxiously sought it because that was *then and there the custom of the church*, and canon-ically required, and consequently, without it—in his own apprehension at least—he was not likely to suc-ceed so well. That bishops were then regarded in the Church of Rome as superior to presbyters in jurisdic-tion, and by the ecclesiastical custom and canons, there is no doubt   But that they are so *jure divino*, by *divine* institution, remained an unsettled question in that Church, even down to the Council of Trent in the six-teenth century, as any one may see in the long and animated debates upon it, as related by Paul Sarpi, the very able and interesting historian of that renowned assembly.

As to Dr. C.'s strictures on Lord King, it is not necessary to follow him through the various items which he
names in that part of his book, in which he repeats
often, as is common with him, what he had previously
affirmed again and again In the very outset of his
strictures he falls into the fundamental error which logicians denominate *ignoratio elenchi*, a mistake of the
question. "Mr. Wesley [he says] professes in his
letter to Mr Asbury, &c , of 1784, to have founded his
belief of the sameness of the office of presbyter and
bishop on the arguments of Lord King in his Inquiry
into the Constitution, &c , of the Primitive Church "*
Now Mr. Wesley says no such thing ; he made no such
profession : and this single observation, so far as Mr.
Wesley is concerned, overthrows the whole of what
Dr C builds on this erroneous foundation ; the pure
fiction of his own imagination.

"Ibi omnis effusus labor."

What Mr Wesley does say in his letter "to Dr.
Coke," &c , is as follows : " Lord King's account of the
primitive church convinced me, many years ago, that
bishops and presbyters are the same order " Mark, the
same *order*, not the same *office*, as Dr. C. asserts of Mr.
Wesley's belief The superiority of bishops in " *degree*,"
or official pre-eminence, though not in essential sacerdotal *order*, is carefully and explicitly marked by Lord
King in many places of his work, and could not have
been overlooked, or intended to be confounded, by Mr.
Wesley Dr C , however, obviously builds his fabric
on the erroneous assumption that both Lord King and
Mr. W made no distinction between ministerial *order*,
strictly taken in its technical ecclesiastical sense, and
office, grade, or *degree*, in an order,—as, for example,
archpresbyters among presbyters, or archdeacons among

* Page 150

deacons, or, to repeat a civil illustration, before mentioned, as the speaker of the House of Commons,—officially superior, and occupying the first seat, and yet but a commoner among commoners

That Dr. C. confounds or overlooks this distinction, and that his argument consequently does not meet Lord King's main position, and of course Mr. W.'s, is plain from several passages in his strictures, but especially from the following.—"Lord King [he says] has entirely passed over the objection to his doctrine arising out of the ordination of bishops   Ordination to an office conveys the idea of introduction into one which the person previously did not hold   If presbyter and bishop was the same office, grade, or order, why were presbyters ordained when they were appointed to a bishoprick? What was the second ordination for?"*

Here he evidently speaks of office, grade, or order as all one and the same thing, and as so treated in Lord King's work   And yet nothing is plainer in the express and frequently repeated language of that author, than that the distinction he makes between *order* and official *grade* or *degree* is the very groundwork of his system.   The question, therefore, which Dr. C so confidently asks, viz, "What was the second ordination for?" is answered with perfect ease and consistency, on the principles of Lord King and Mr. W., and equally on those of the polity of the Methodist Episcopal Church. Dr C. himself, indeed, furnishes the answer to his own question, and nothing can be more appropriate or correct: "Ordination to an office [he says] conveys the idea of introduction into one which the person previously did not hold."*   Exactly so.   This is the precise import of ordination as understood by Lord K, and also by Mr. W and the Methodist Episcopal Church And therefore, while Lord K explicitly maintains the primitive identity of bishops and presbyters as to the

* Page 176.

intrinsic and inherent power of *order*, he as explicitly states, at the same time, that when a presbyter was advanced to the *official degree* of bishop—that is, according to Lord K , was made the actual superintendent, inspector, or overseer of any particular church, and of his fellow presbyters (as well as the deacons) connected therewith,—he was *ordained* to that office by imposition of hands by the neighbouring bishops   But when he says " by the neighbouring *bishops*," the reader must not forget that he still does not at all mean *diocesan bishops* of a *distinct order*, in Dr C 's or the high church sense ; but in *his own* sense of the term *bishop*, as above described.*   The same answer, furnished by Dr. C. himself, may very clearly explain to him and to all others why it is that the Methodist Episcopal Church, which maintains the identity of bishop and presbyter as to the intrinsic and inherent power of *order*, still practises a third ordination, when any of her presbyters are advanced to the episcopal degree   It is exactly because, in Dr. C.'s own words, " ordination to an office conveys the idea of introduction into one which the person previously did not hold "

Having thus cleared the true idea both of the order and the official degree of bishop, as held by Lord King, by Mr. W , and by the Methodist Episcopal Church, and the true basis on which, in accordance with this idea, an appropriate ordination to the episcopal office rests, I shall proceed to give the reader a brief synopsis of Lord K 's argumentation and deductions from the Christian fathers of the first three centuries, to which he confines his inquiry on the main point in question, viz , the primitive identity of the order of bishops and presbyters And in the course of it, I am persuaded the intelligent and candid reader cannot but be as forcibly struck with the *modesty* as with the *learned diligence* of that distin-

---

* See his " Inquiry into the Constitution, Discipline, Unity, and Worship of the Primitive Church," p 49.

guished layman, whose authorities and logical deductions were capable of producing so great a change in
the previously prejudiced high-church mind of such a
man as Wesley.   It will serve also to show how little
justice has been done by Dr C. to this main point of
Lord K's argument.   It may be proper, first, however,
to apprize the reader that Lord King actually and carefully read and studied the early fathers whom he
quotes, and various others, in the Greek and Latin ori-
ginals, and not in translations, nor "*by the index,*" as
seems to be Dr. C.'s plan of *discovering* passages *

In his sixth chapter, Lord King says "It will be both
needless and tedious to endeavour to prove that the ancients generally mention presbyters distinct from bishops
Every one, I suppose, will readily own and acknowledge it   The great question which hath most deplo-
rably sharpened and soured the minds of too many is,
what the office and order of a presbyter was. about this
the world hath been and still is most uncharitably
divided, some equalize a presbyter in every thing with
a bishop; others as much debase him, each, according to
their particular opinions, either advance or degrade him.
In many controversies a middle way hath been the
safest, perhaps in this, the medium between the two ex-
treams may be the truest   Whether what I am now
going to say be the true state of the matter, I leave
to the learned reader to determin; I may be deceived,
—neither mine years nor abilities exempt me from mistakes and errors, but this I must needs say, That after
the most diligent researches and impartialest inquiries,
the following notion seems to me most plausible, and
most consentaneous to truth : and which, with a great
facility and clearness, solves those doubts and objections which, according to those other hypotheses, I
know not how to answer   But yet, however, I am not
so wedded and bigoted to this opinion, but if any shall

* Page 161

produce better and more convincing arguments to the contrary, I will not contentiously defend, but readily relinquish it, since I search after truth, not to promote a particular party or interest

"Now for the better explication of this point, I shall first lay down a definition and description of a presbyter, and then prove the parts thereof.

"Now the definition of a presbyter may be this:— *A person in holy orders, having thereby an inherent right to perform the whole office of a bishop; but being possessed of no place or parish, not actually discharging it, without the permission and consent of the bishop of a place or parish.*

"But lest this definition should seem obscure, I shall illustrate it by this following instance As a curate hath the same mission and power with the minister whose place he supplies, yet being not the minister of that place, he cannot perform there any acts of his ministerial function without leave from the minister thereof, so a presbyter had the same order and power with a bishop, whom he assisted in his cure ; yet being not the bishop or minister of that cure, he could not there perform any parts of his pastoral office, without the permission of the bishop thereof: so that what we generally render bishops, priests, and deacons, would be more intelligible in our tongue if we did express it by rectors, vicars, and deacons,—by rectors understanding the bishops, and by vicars the presbyters ; the former being the actual incumbents of a place, and the latter curates or assistants, and so different in degree but yet equal in order.

"Now this is what I understand by a presbyter; for the confirmation of which these two things are to be proved .

"I. That the presbyters were the bishops' curates and assistants, and so inferiour to them in the actual exercise of their ecclesiastical commission.

"II That yet, notwithstanding, they had the same inherent right with the bishops, and so were not of a distinct specific order from them Or, more briefly, thus,

"1 That the presbyters were different from the bishops *in gradu*, or *in degree*, but yet,

"2 They were equal to them *in ordine*, or *in order*.

"As to the first of these, that presbyters were but the bishops' curates and assistants, inferior to them in degree, or in the actual discharge of their ecclesiastical commission; this will appear to have been in effect already proved, if we recollect what has been asserted touching the bishop and his office —that there was but one bishop in a church, that he usually performed all the parts of divine service, that he was the general disposer and manager of all things within his diocess, there being nothing done there without his consent and approbation "*

He then specifies the various particulars of ministerial functions which a presbyter could not perform without the bishop's leave, adding at the close —"But what need I reckon up particulars, when in general there was no ecclesiastical office performed by the presbyters without the consent and permission of the bishop "†

Having cited his authorities for these statements, he afterward thus proceeds :—

"So then in this sense a presbyter was inferior to a bishop in degree, in that, having no parish of his own, he could not actually discharge the particular acts of his ministerial function without leave from the bishop of a parish or diocess The bishops were superior to the presbyters in that they were the presented, instituted, and inducted ministers of their respective parishes ; and the presbyters were inferior to the bishops in that they were but their curates and assistants

* Inquiry, &c , pp 52–55   † Page 56.

8

"§ 3 But though the presbyters were thus different from the bishops in degree, yet they were of the very same specific order with them, having the same inherent right to perform those ecclesiastical offices which the bishop did, as will appear from these three arguments:

"1 That by the bishop's permission they discharged all those offices which a bishop did —2, that they were called by the same titles and appellations as the bishops were.—and, 3, that they are expressly said to be of the same order with the bishops. As to the first of these, That by the bishop's permission they discharged all those offices which a bishop did,—this will appear from that,

"1. When the bishop ordered them they preached Thus Origen, in the beginning of some of his sermons, tells us that he was commanded thereunto by the bishop, as particularly when he preached about the witch of *Endor*, he says, *The bishop commanded him to do it.*

"2. By the permission of the bishop presbyters baptized. Thus writes Tertullian,—*The bishop has the right of baptizing, and then the presbyters, but not without his leave.*

"3 By the leave of the bishop presbyters administered the eucharist, as must be supposed in that saying of Ignatius, 'That that eucharist only was valid which was celebrated by the bishop, or by one appointed by him, and that the eucharist could not be delivered but by the bishop, or by one whom he did approve.'

"4 The presbyters ruled in those churches to which they belonged,—else this exhortation of Polycarpus to the presbyters of Philippi would have been in vain: 'Let the presbyters be tender and merciful, compassionate towards all, reducing those that are in errors, visiting all that are weak, not negligent of the widow and the orphan, and him that is poor, but ever providing what is honest in the sight of God and man, abstaining from all wrath, respect of persons, and unrighteous judg-

8*

ment, being far from covetousness, not hastily believing a report against any man, not rigid in judgment, knowing that we are all faulty and obnoxious to judgment' Hence,

"5. They presided in church consistories, together with the bishop, and composed the executive part of the ecclesiastical court, from whence it was called the *presbytery*, because in it, as Tertullian says, 'Approved elders did preside'

"6 They had also the power of excommunication, as Rogatianus and Numidicus, two presbyters of Cyprian's church, by his order joined with some bishops of his nomination in the excommunication of certain schismatics of his diocess   But of both these two heads more will be spoken in another place.

"7. Presbyters restored returning penitents to the church's peace   Thus we read, in an epistle of Dionysius, bishop of Alexandria, that a certain offender called Serapion, approaching to the time of his dissolution, 'sent for one of the presbyters to absolve him, which the presbyter did according to the order of his bishop, who had before commanded that the presbyters should absolve those who were in danger of death'

"8 Presbyters confirmed, as we shall most evidently prove when we come to treat of confirmation, only remark here by the way, that in the days of Cyprian there was a hot controversy whether those that were baptized by heretics, and came over to the catholic church, should be received as members thereof by baptism and confirmation, or by confirmation alone   Now I would fain know, whether, during the vacancy of a see, or the bishop's absence, which sometimes might be very long, as Cyprian was absent two years, a presbyter could not admit a returning heretic to the peace and unity of the church, especially if we consider their positive damnation of all those that died out of the church. If the presbyters had not had this power of confirmation, many penitent souls must have been damned for the unavoidable default of a bishop, which is too cruel and unjust to imagine.

"9 As for ordination, I find but little said of this in antiquity, yet, as little as there is, there are clearer proofs of the presbyters ordaining, than there are of their administering the Lord's supper. 'All power and grace,' saith Firmilian, 'is constituted in the church, where seniors preside, who have the power of baptizing, confirming, and ordaining;' or, as it may be rendered, and perhaps more agreeable to the sense of the place,— 'who had the power as of baptizing, so also of confirming and ordaining' What these seniors were will be best understood by a parallel place in Tertullian, for that place in Tertullian and this in Firmilian are usually cited to expound one another by most learned men, as the most learned Dr Cave and others Now the passage in Tertullian is this,—'In the ecclesiastical courts approved elders preside' Now by these approved elders bishops and presbyters must necessarily be understood. Because Tertullian speaks here of the discipline exerted in one particular church or parish, in which there was but one bishop ; and if only he had presided, then there could not have been elders in the plural number, but there being many elders to make out their number, we must add the presbyters to the bishop, who also presided with him, as we shall more fully show in another place Now the same that presided in church consistories, the same also ordained Presbyters as well as bishops presided in church consistories, therefore presbyters as well as bishops ordained And as in those churches where there were presbyters, both they and the bishop presided together, so also they ordained together, both laying on their hands in ordination, as St. Timothy was ordained 'by the laying on of the hands of the presbytery.' that is, by the hands of the bishop and presbyters of that parish where he was ordained,—as is the constant signification of the word, *presbytery* in all the writings of the ancients. But,

"10 Though as to every particular act of the bishop's office, it could not be proved particularly that a presbyter did discharge them ; yet it would be sufficient if we could prove that in the general a presbyter could and did perform them all.—Now that a presbyter could do so, and consequently, by the bishop's permission, did do so, will appear from the example of the great St Cyprian, bishop of Carthage, who, being exiled from his church, writes a letter to the clergy thereof, wherein he exhorts and begs them 'to discharge their own and his office too, that so nothing might be wanting either to discipline or diligence.' And much to the same effect he thus writes them in another letter, *Trusting, therefore, to your kindness and religion, which I have abundantly experienced, I exhort and command you by these letters, that in my stead you perform those offices which the ecclesiastical dispensation requires* And in a letter written upon the same occasion by the clergy of the church of Rome to the clergy of the church of Carthage, we find these words toward the beginning thereof. *And since it is incumbent upon us, who are as it were bishops, to keep the flock in the room of the pastor · if we shall be found negligent, it shall be said unto us as it was said to our careless preceding bishops,* in Ezekiel xxxiv, 3, 4, *that we looked not after that which was lost, we did not correct him that wandered, nor bound up him that was lame, but we did eat their milk and were covered with their wool* So that the presbyters were, as it were, bishops, that in the bishop's absence kept his flock, and in his stead performed all those ecclesiastical offices which were incumbent on him

"Now then, if the presbyters could supply the place of an absent bishop, and in general discharge all those offices to which a bishop had been obliged if he had been present, it naturally follows that the presbyters could discharge every particular act and part thereof If I should say, such an one has all the senses of a man, and yet also assert that he cannot see, I should be judged a self-contradictor in that assertion; for in affirming that he had all the human senses, I also affirmed that he saw, because seeing is one of those senses,—for whatsoever is affirmed of an universal, is affirmed of every one of its particulars So when the fathers say that the presbyters performed the whole office of the bishop, it naturally ensues that they confirmed, ordained, baptized, &c., because those are particulars of that universal.

"But now, from the whole, we may collect a solid argument for the equality of presbyters with bishops, as to order; for if a presbyter did all a bishop did, what difference was there between them ? A bishop preached, baptized, and confirmed , so did a presbyter.   A bishop excommunicated, absolved, and ordained , so did a presbyter.   Whatever a bishop the same did a presbyter. The particular acts of their office were the same , the only difference that was between them was in degree, —but this proves there was none at all in order.

"That bishops and presbyters were of the same order appears also from that originally they had one and the same name, each of them being indifferently called bishops or presbyters.   Hence we read in the Sacred Writ of several bishops in one particular church, as the *bishops of Ephesus* and *Philippi,* that is, the bishops and presbyters of those churches, as they were afterward distinctly called   And Clemens Romanus sometimes mentions many bishops in the church of Corinth whom at other times he calls by the name of presbyters, using those two terms as synonymous titles and appellations '*You have obeyed,*' saith he, '*those that were set over you,* τοις ηγουμενοις ημων, and *let us revere those that are set over us,*' προηγουμενους ημων, which are the usual titles of the bishops, and yet these in another place he calls *presbyters,* describing their office by *their sitting or presiding over us*   Wherefore he commands the Corinthians to be subject to their *presbyters,* and whom in

one line he calls επισκοποι, or bishops ; the second line
after he calls πρεσβυτεροι, or presbyters So *Polycarp*
exhorts the *Philippians to be subject to their presbyters
and deacons,*—under the name of presbyters including
both bishops and priests, as we now call them

"The first that expressed these church officers by
the distinct terms of bishops and presbyters was Ignatius, who lived in the beginning of the second century,
appropriating the title of bishop, επισκοπος, or overseer, to
that minister who was the more immediate overseer and
governor of his parish , and that of πρεσβυτερος, elder or
presbyter, to him who had no particular care and inspection of a parish, but was only an assistant or curate
to a bishop that had . the word επισκοπος, or bishop, denoting a relation to a flock or cure ; πρεσβυτερος, or presbyter, signifying only a power or ability to take the
charge of such a flock or cure,—the former implying
an actual discharge of the office, the latter a power so
to do

" This distinction of titles, arising from the difference
of their circumstances, which we find first mentioned
in Ignatius, was generally followed by the succeeding
fathers, who for the most part distinguish between
bishops and presbyters, though sometimes, according to
the primitive usage, they indifferently apply those terms
to each of those persons.   Thus, on the one hand, the
titles of presbyters are given unto bishops, as Irenæus
in his synodical epistle twice calls Anicetus, Pius, Higy-
nus, Telesphorus, and Sixtus, bishops of Rome. πρεσβυτεροι,
or presbyters   And those bishops who derived their
succession immediately from the apostles he calls the
presbyters in the church and whom Clemens Alexandrinus in one line calls the bishop of a certain city not
far from Ephesus, a few lines after he calls the presbyter   And on the other hand, the titles of bishops are
ascribed to presbyters, as one of the discretive appellations of a bishop is pastor.   Yet Cyprian also calls his

presbyters the pastors of the flock.   Another was that
of president, or one set over the people   Yet Cyprian
also calls his presbyters presidents, or set over the people   The bishops were also called rectors or rulers .
so Origen calls the presbyters the governors of the
people.   And we find both bishops and presbyters included under the common name of presidents or prelates
by St. Cyprian, in this his exhortation to Pomponius
'And if all must observe the divine discipline, how much
more must the presidents and deacons do it, who by
their conversation and manners must yield a good example to others?'   Now if the same appellation of a
thing be a good proof for the identity of its nature, then
bishops and presbyters must be of the same order, because they had the same names and titles   Suppose it
was disputed whether a parson and lecturer were of the
same order, would not this sufficiently prove the affirmative ?   That though for some accidental respects they
might be distinguished in their appellations, yet originally and frequently they were called by one and the
same name   The same it is in this case, though for
some contingent and adventitious reasons, bishops and
presbyters were discriminated in their titles, yet originally they were always, and afterward sometimes, called
by one and the same appellation, and therefore we may
justly deem them to be one and the same order   But
if this reason be not thought cogent enough, the third
and last will unquestionably put all out of doubt, and
most clearly evince the identity or sameness of bishops
and presbyters as to order   And that is, that it is expressly said by the ancients that there were but two
distinct ecclesiastical orders, viz , bishops and deacons,
or presbyters and deacons ; and if there were but these
two, presbyters cannot be distinct from bishops, for then
there would be three.

"Now that there were but two orders, viz , bishops
and deacons, is plain from that golden ancient remain of

Clemens Romanus, wherein he thus writes —'In the country and cities where the apostles preached, they ordained their first converts for bishops and deacons over those who should believe Nor were these orders new, for, for many ages past it was thus prophesied concerning bishops and deacons I will appoint their bishops in righteousness, and their deacons in faith' This place of Scripture which is here quoted is in Isa lx, 17. 'I will make thine officers peace and thine exactors righteousness.' Whether it is rightly applied, is not my business to determine. That that I observe from hence is, that there were but two orders instituted by the apostles, viz, bishops and deacons, which Clemens supposes were prophetically promised long before "*

He then quotes a farther passage from the same epistle of Clemens to the Corinthians, the object of which was to dissuade an unruly faction in that church from a design which they entertained of deposing their presbyters The great argument of Clemens to this end was, that they ought rather to obey their presbyters, and to desist from their disorderly proceedings against them, because the institution and succession of bishops and deacons was from the apostles themselves, which, continues Lord K, "clearly evinces that presbyters were included under the title of bishops, or rather, that they were bishops For to what end should Clemens exhort the schismatical Corinthians to obey their presbyters, from the consideration of the apostles' ordination of bishops, if their presbyters had not been bishops? But that the order of presbyters was the same with the order of bishops, will appear also from that place of Irenæus, where he exhorts us ' to withdraw from those presbyters who serve their lusts, and, having not the fear of God in their hearts, contemn others, and are lifted up with the dignity of their first session ; but to adhere to those

* Inquiry, &c , p 57–69

who keep the doctrine of the apostles, and with their presbyterial order are inoffensive and exemplary in sound doctrine and a holy conversation, to the information and correction of others ; for such presbyters the church educates, and of whom the prophet saith, I will give thee princes in peace, and bishops in righteousness '

"Now that by these presbyters bishops are meant, I need not take much pains to prove, the precedent chapter positively asserts it, the description of them in this quotation, by their enjoying the dignity of the first session, and the application of that text of Isaiah unto them, clearly evinces it   No one can deny but that they were bishops, that is, that they were superior in degree to other presbyters, or, as Irenæus styles it, honoured with the first session ; but yet he also says that they were not different in order, being of the presbyterial order, which includes both bishops and presbyters "*

After quoting next a passage from Clemens Alexandrinus, in proof or illustration of the same point, he thus proceeds .—

" So that there were only the two orders of deacons and presbyters, the former whereof being the inferior order, never sat at their ecclesiastical conventions, but, like servants, *stood* and waited on the latter, who *sat* down on Θρονοι, or seats in the form of a semicircle, whence they are frequently called consessus presbyterii, or the session of the presbytery, in which session he that was more peculiarly the bishop or minister of the parish sat at the head of the semicircle on a seat somewhat elevated above those of 'his colleagues,' as Cyprian calls them ; and so was distinguished from them by his priority in the same order, but not by his being of another order.   Thus the foresaid Clemens Alexandrinus distinguishes the bishop from the presbyters by his being

* Inquiry, pp 71, 72.

advanced to the πρωτοκαθεδρια, or the first seat in the presbytery, not by his sitting in a different seat from them — For he thus writes, 'He is in truth a presbyter of the church and a minister of the will of God, who does and teaches the things of the Lord, not ordained by men or esteemed just because a presbyter, but because just, therefore received into the presbytery,—who, although he be not honoured with the first seat on earth, yet shall hereafter sit down on the twenty and four thrones mentioned in the Revelations, judging the people' So that both bishops and presbyters were members of the same presbytery, only the bishop was advanced to the first and chiefest seat therein,—which is the very same with what I come now from proving, *viz*, that bishops and presbyters were equal in order but different in degree: that the former were ministers of their respective parishes, and the latter then curates or assistants

"Whether this hath been fully proved, or whether the precedent quotations do naturally conclude the premises, the learned reader will easily determine I am not conscious that I have stretched any words beyond their natural signification ; having deduced from them nothing but what they fairly imported If I am mistaken I hope I shall be pardoned, since I did it not designedly or voluntarily As before, so now I profess again, that if any one shall be so kind and obliging to give me better information, I shall thankfully and willingly acknowledge and quit mine error; but till that information be given, and the falsity of my present opinion be evinced, (which after the impartialest and narrowest inquiry I see not how it can be done,) I hope no one will be offended that I have asserted the equality or identity of the bishops and presbyters as to order, and their difference as to pre-eminency or degree.

" § 4 Now from this notion of presbyters there evidently results the reason why there were many of them in one church, even for the same intent and end, though more necessary and needful, that curates are now to those ministers and incumbents whom they serve, it was found by experience that variety of accidents and circumstances did frequently occur both in times of peace and persecution, the particulars whereof would be needless to enumerate, that disabled the bishops from attending on, and discharging their pastoral office; therefore that such vacancies might be supplied, and such inconveniences remedied, they entertained presbyters or curates, who during their absence might supply their places, who also were helpful to them whilst they were present with their flocks, to counsel and advise them Whence Bishop *Cyprian* assures us that he did all things by the common counsel of his presbyters.

"Besides this, in those early days of Christianity, churches were in most places thin, and at great distances from one another ; so that if a bishop by any disaster was incapacitated for the discharge of his function, it would be very difficult to get a neighbouring bishop to assist him To which we may also add, that in those times there were no public schools or universities, except we say the catechetic lecture at *Alexandria* was one for the breeding of young ministers, who might succeed the bishops as they died , wherefore the bishops of every church took care to instruct and elevate some young men, who might be prepared to come in their place when they were dead and gone And thus, for these and the like reasons, most churches were furnished with a competent number of presbyters, who helped the bishops while living, and were fitted to succeed them when dead "*

Into the next sentiment advanced by Lord King, he seems to have been led by an erroneous reading of a passage in the edition of Tertullian's works which he used, and which I find corrected in one of Dr Camp-

* Inquiry, pp. 74–77.

bell's lectures on Ecclesiastical History, p 121   The passage as quoted by Lord K is,—" Ubi ecclesiastici ordinis non est consessus, et offert, et tingit sacerdos, qui est ibi solus " *Exhort ad Castitat* p 457.   And from it he deduces the sentiment that although most churches were furnished with presbyters, yet that this was not essential , a bishop being sufficient, &c   Dr. Campbell says a bishop and "some deacons"   The latter is not added by Lord King, but Dr. Campbell shall speak for himself

"Some have inferred from a passage of Tertullian that, however general the practice was in the second and subsequent centuries, of settling in every church all the three orders above explained, it was not universal , that in parishes where there were but a few Christians remotely situated from other churches, it was judged sufficient to give them a pastor or bishop only and some deacons   The presbyter then being but a sort of assistant to the bishop, might not, in very small charges, be judged necessary   The thing is not in itself improbable, and the authority above-mentioned, before I had examined it or seen a more accurate edition, led me to conclude it real.   But on examination I find that what had drawn me and others into this opinion was no more than a false reading of a sentence quoted in a former lecture   In some editions of Tertullian we read, (*De Exhort. Cast.*,) ' Ubi ecclesiastici ornis non est consessus, et offert, et tinguit, sacerdos qui est ibi solus.'   I need not urge that the expression is quite different in all the best manuscripts and most correct editions : this being one of those glaring corruptions which, after a careful perusal, betray themselves to an attentive reader of any penetration   The words, as I have now transcribed them, considered in connection with the subject treated in the context, have neither sense nor coherence in them, whereas, nothing can be more apposite to the author's argument than they are in the way formerly quoted, 'Ubi ecclesiastici ordinis non est consessus, et offers, et tinguis, et sacerdos es tibi solus.' So sensible of this were the two learned critics Petavius and Dodwell, that though both were violently disposed, in their different ways, to pervert the meaning, neither thought proper to avail himself of a variation in the reading which would have removed at once what to them was a great stumbling-block. It is indeed a reading which savours more of art than of negligence, and has much the appearance of those inquisitorial corrections which were made on several ancient books in the sixteenth century, especially those published in the papal dominions, or where the holy office was established, in order to adapt the ancient doctrine to the orthodoxy of the day. Now nothing could be more opposite to this, than what seemed to admit that any necessity or exigence whatever could entitle a layman to exercise the function of a priest "*

A few miscellaneous specimens of Dr. C.'s criticisms on Lord K. shall conclude my notice of this part of his book.

" As for the word *diocess*, [says Lord K,] by which the bishop's flock is now usually expressed, I do not remember that ever I found it used in this sense by any of the ancients "† On this passage Dr. C remarks as follows —" Socrates, however, who lived in the fourth century, in his account of the Council of Constantinople, says they decreed that the bishop of a *diocess, diœcesis*, should not pass (be translated) to another church — The word occurs twice more within the compass of a page It is evident from its being used in the wording of a law or canon that it was common and well understood "‡

The Council of Constantinople was held about fifteen years before the *close* of the *fourth* century , and So-

* Lect on Ecclesiastical History, pp 121, 122. † Inquiry, p 15 ‡ Page 153

crates consequently must have written still later   Dr C. knew that Lord K 's inquiry was expressly confined to the writers of the *first three centuries*   Yet he says that a word which Lord K. did not remember to have seen, in the sense mentioned, in any writer of the first three centuries, may be found in three instances in a writer nearly *a hundred years later*, and he *infers* from its being once used in a law about that time, that it was *then* common and well understood.   Does this, were it even so, disprove any thing that Lord K had said ?

One of Lord King's sentiments was, that the ancient bishoprics were the same as modern parishes, under the proper pastoral care of the bishop, though they might have been larger in extent of territory, or have covered a greater space of ground.   In descanting on this topic, Dr. C., to show his view of the subject, selects the church of Jerusalem, among others, as a specimen of the extent of the ancient churches.   And as we have authentic accounts of that church in the only certain church history extant,—the Acts of the Apostles,—I will [subject] Dr. C.'s strictures for a moment to the test of that record *

Among all the writers I have yet looked into, I must say that I have seldom or never met with one who so frequently and so coolly avails himself of the *petitio principii* (begging the question) as Dr C   Lord King, in proof of his position that presbyters ordained, adduces a passage from Firmilian above quoted   On which Dr C, after a train of other remarks, makes the following :—" But when, in addition to these considerations we have Firmilian's own declaration that in his epistle he is speaking of bishops, contest is at an end "† How at an end ?   Is it not the very position of Lord K , sustained by other eminent critics, that the writers of

---

* [The author appears to have intended to insert here a criticism of this kind, which he had previously written   It will be found in the Appendix, as it could not well be introduced here —Ed]   † Page 173

that period frequently use the terms bishop and presbyter interchangeably,—calling the same persons indifferently by one or the other name? But Dr C's mind seems so engrossed with the notion that bishop can be no other than a high church diocesan, that wherever the word occurs, this idea seems with him a matter of course. The following may be given as an instance — the phrase "*majores natu*" in Firmilian is rendered by Lord K "seniors," or, according to the parallel phrase, "*probati seniores;*" in Tertullian, "approved elders." and that these approved elders, for reasons which Lord K. assigns, included both bishops and presbyters, he says "must necessarily be understood "* On this statement of Lord K 's, Dr C thus argues —

"It is furthermore to be observed that all Lord King urges on this passage is, that *majores natu* included both the bishop and his presbyters, and that *both they and the bishop* ordained together, both laying on their hands in ordination, as Timothy was ordained by the laying on of the hands of the presbytery that is, by the hands of the bishop and presbyters of that parish where he was ordained, as is the constant signification of the word *presbytery* in all the writings of the ancients" (Page 62, part i.) By his own account, therefore, a bishop was present at the ordination of Timothy, spoken of in Paul's first epistle to him, and "Paul must have been that bishop."† The reader will observe that his affirmation is, that as a bishop was present, according to Lord K 's "own account," it follows of course and necessarily that "*Paul must* have been that bishop" And yet nothing is plainer than that, according to Lord K , the bishop was the pastor of that particular church where Timothy was ordained, who, together with the presbyters connected with him in the same church, constituted its "presbytery"

On leaving Lord King Dr. C. descends at once to the age of the Reformation. And in this field it is wonderful with what facility he puts to flight whole hosts of "men of first-rate talents and learning," as he is compelled to admit they were .* and by a few simple dashes of his own more learned, more fearless, or more honest pen, demolishes at once the fair fame of the immortal band who jeoparded their lives and every earthly interest to rescue Christendom " from the tyranny of the bishop of Rome and all his detestable enormities," as the English reformed litany originally expressed it

To the admission of the validity of ordination by presbyters, on the part of many of the most distinguished episcopal writers and dignitaries, both "during the progress of the reformation and since," Dr. C replies, that at most it was but their opinion formed upon various considerations —in some, from affection for individuals of the continental reformers , in others, perhaps in *all* of the early English reformers, from *fear* of the consequences of breaking with the non-episcopal churches ; that some "were not Episcopalians in principle, [not of Dr C's "stamp" certainly,] but were secretly plotting to subvert the order of the church " that " even some *bishops* were *suspected* of being opposed to it ;" and finally, that "*all* were more or less influenced by the *fear* of breaking with the continental reformers "†—So that in *all* of them, according to Dr C , this pusillanimous motive operated either to impair their intellect, or else to destroy their integrity in a matter which, on his scheme, is essential to the very being of the Christian church ' Even the amiable and *truly apostolical and Christian* spirit which breathed in the breast of the magnanimous *Usher*,—who avowed that although he deemed those churches which had no bishops defective in government, yet that he loved and honoured them as true members of the universal church, and that, were

* Page 179.   † Page 178.

9

he in Holland, he would receive the blessed sacrament at the hands of the Dutch with the like affection that he would from the hands of the French minister, were he at Clarenton,*—even this illustrious primate's motives must fall under Dr C's imputation of weakness or of dishonesty   Nay, the no less amiable and equally apostolical and Christian spirit of the continental reformers, who received the English episcopal fugitives from the terrors of bloody Mary "with the utmost cordiality," and treated them " with the greatest friendship and hospitality," in passing through Dr C's alembic, is strangely transmuted into an auxiliary of his cause. One would suppose, if the characteristics of discipleship established by the Master are to be regarded, that it ought to be considered rather as a proof of the Christian genuineness of churches whose leaders and members breathed such a spirit —"By this shall all men know that ye are my disciples, if ye have love one to another:"† a testimony worth ten thousand "passages," genuine or spurious, from St Ignatius, or any other uninspired saint.   This spirit, which *reciprocally* animated the English and continental churches, in their official and ministerial intercourse with each other, in those golden days of mutual and joint resistance to high church and popery, Dr C's doctrine would and does, at this day, banish from the earth   It is the doctrine of thorough sectarian bigotry and Scriptural schism   For what is schism, in the true Scriptural sense, but the alienation of Christians from each other *in heart*   And if this be its genuine import, as, on the authority of inspiration, we affirm it is, then whose doctrine, tested by this infallible criterion, is most schismatical, that of Usher, or that of Dr C ?   In other words, whose is most hostile or friendly to that fundamental principle of Christianity among Christians and churches, —mutual love ? whose tends most to conciliate their

---

* Letter to Dr. Bernard   † John xiii. 35.

affections where differences have unhappily arisen, or, by means of uncharitable and dogmatical decisions to widen the breach, and hinder their reciprocal recognition and ecclesiastical intercourse? Where the former spirit prevails, it is Christian, where the latter, it is schismatical

I know that Dr C. is pleased to say, that it is " far from being the desire of those who believe that episcopal [high church] ordination alone is valid, to prevent any qualified person from entering into the ministry."— And that "they only wish" them to "obtain that" " authority" "which is" valid * That is to say, in effect, "Master, we saw one casting out devils in thy name, and we forbad him, *because he followeth not us*" The answer of Jesus is our answer. If the reader please he may look at it, Mark ix, 38, and Luke ix, 49. Can any be so blind as not to discern the very spirit of the sectary lurking under the cloak of Dr. C.'s apparent liberality?†

I find little in the remaining part of Dr C's work that is worthy of observation What he says in reference to Mr. W. and on the Scripture argument, will be noticed hereafter ‡ It would seem, indeed, according to Dr C, that not only the Scriptures, and all the ancient Christian writers, but even the master spirits among the continental reformers, (from *fear* of whom, mark it, according to the same Dr C, or from affection for whom, the English episcopal reformers had proved recreant to their own principles and to their church, many of them having been corrupted in this respect by the great hospitality and friendship of those said continental reform-

* Pages 147, 148.

† [Here is a note in the MS indicating that the author intended to insert an extract from something which he had previously written To avoid confusion, it is given in the Appendix —Ed]

‡ [Never accomplished, except so far as the Scripture argument is taken up in his reply to Dr Onderdonk, at the close of this book —Ed.]

ers during an actual residence among them!) are in favour of the high church scheme   Now this is really passing strange   That they should have been in sentiment and in heart at least decided Episcopalians themselves, and yet, not only by their public acts and writings, but in their intimate, social, and confidential personal intercourse, have so greatly and so injuriously influenced episcopalians against episcopacy!   The inconsistency of these opposite grounds, both taken by Dr C , is so manifest and glaring, that I am driven to the conclusion that he mistakes his men and mistakes their meaning   The continental reformers, in a noble and commendable reciprocation of the truly Christian and enlightened spirit of the English episcopal reformers, undoubtedly admitted the *lawfulness* of episcopacy, and in certain circumstances its expediency and high utility   That there was nothing in it, when properly understood, inconsistent with gospel principles or apostolical precept or example —that it had in fact, prevailed in the church generally from a very early period, if not from the days of the apostles ; and that, from these considerations there was nothing in it, thus understood, to offend a good conscience or to require separation from episcopal communion   That those of them who went the farthest meant nothing more, is evident from Dr. C 's own selected passages from Grotius himself, of whom he makes the largest and strongest use   I need not here repeat what has been so often mentioned by others, that Grotius is believed to have become somewhat soured by the ill treatment he received from the Presbyterian churches of Holland   His own language, as quoted by Dr. C himself, is sufficient for my present purpose.   The very title of one of the sections of Grotius, from which Dr C takes a number of his quotations, is, " *The episcopal superiority is not of Divine command* "   This proposition he then proceeds to establish by a variety of arguments, and explicitly asserts

that what he thus alleges for "the equality of pastors"
is "not at all repugnant to the former,"—that is, to
what he had before said on the subject of episcopacy.
He shows plainly also, that he understood Jerome in
the sense which has been herein represented, and that
he himself adopted the same views. "Jerome says,
[remarks Grotius,] *The bishops became greater than the
presbyters, more by custom than by the truth of the Divine ordering*" He quotes St Augustine, bishop of
Hippo in the same century, to the same effect, as follows: "*The episcopate is greater than the presbyterate
in the name of honour which the practice of the church
hath retained*" Epist. xix   He admits indeed that when
the fathers speak of "custom," they do not exclude that
of the apostolical age itself: but contends at the same
time that not every apostolical institution or practice
is therefore necessarily of Divine command; of which
he alleges several instances, and then continues thus.—
" Add also, that the apostles so instituted bishops, that
they left certain churches without bishops: Epiphanius
acknowledges this —*There was need of presbyters and
deacons, for by these two the ecclesiastical offices could be
fulfilled ; but when there was not found any one worthy
of the episcopate, the place remained without a bishop; but
when there was need, and there were persons worthy of the
episcopate, bishops were appointed*   Those churches,
therefore, as Jerome says, *were governed by the common
council of presbyters*"

In his notes on some of the above extracts, Dr. C
makes the assertion that we are not only bound to believe what the apostles taught, but that " what they did
we are bound to practise "*

He observes also, that the apostles did not " command
that the church should be governed by the common

* Page 191 [A note in the MS here, indicates that the author intended
to add some instances to illustrate the absurdity of such a principle   Such,
however, will readily present themselves to the reader —Ed.]

council of presbyters." This is granted, and accordingly and consistently, we maintain, that the presbyterian model of church polity is no more of essential, universal, and perpetual obligation, by Divine right, than high-church episcopacy

If any thing be yet wanting to set Grotius's opinion in a clear light, the following with ordinary persons, though probably not with Dr C , seem to be sufficient "All the ancients [says Grotius] confess that there was no act so peculiarly the bishop's [*confirmation*, of course, included, Dr C to the contrary notwithstanding] that it might not also be exercised by the presbyter, except the right of ordaining" He quotes Chrysostom and *Jerome* to show this, and then adds —"But although the right of ordaining *is taken away from presbyters*, [mark, '*is taken away*,' not that they never possessed it,] according to the opinion of these fathers, which constitution (or law) may be seen in many councils universal and local, [which shows by what means, in his view, the right had been *taken away* from presbyters,] what nevertheless hinders that we may interpret it so that presbyters could ordain no one without the bishop's consent ?"

A little after he says, " Yet I do not see how that can be refuted, where there are not bishops, that ordination might be rightly performed even by a presbyter " And again —"Then, as we have said above, it is doubtful whether presbyters, who neither have presbyters under them nor a bishop over them, belong to (the order of) bishops, or to (that of) mere presbyters For Ambrose thus argues of Timothy,—*he, who had no other before him, was a bishop*. Indeed, (that we may take an example from the republic,) many things are lawful to a senate not having a king, which are not lawful to a senate constituted under a king Because a senate without a king is as it were a king "

The passage of "Ambrose," above alluded to by Grotius, is probably that of *Hilary,* whose works are always bound up with those of Ambrose, and by some blunder in the editors, says Dr Campbell, continue to pass under his name. Dr. C seems also to have taken Hilary as Ambrose The entire passage is one which I cannot but think entirely refutes the efforts made by Dr C in a former part of his work to enlist Hilary in his service It also explains fully the observation which Dr. C so often repeats, on the credit of Hilary, that though every bishop is a presbyter, yet every presbyter is not a bishop The connection and explanation of this very just saying, as given by Hilary himself, Dr. C is careful to omit But the reader shall have it in Hilary's own words, from his Commentary on the third chapter of first Timothy, of which the papal critic Richard Simon says, there are few ancient comments on the epistle of St Paul, and even on the whole New Testament, which can be compared with this. The words are —

"Post episcopum tamen diaconi ordinationem subjecit Quare? nisi quia episcopi et presbyteri una ordinatio est? Uterque enim sacerdos est. Sed episcopus primus est; ut omnis episcopus presbyter sit, non omnis presbyter episcopus Hic enim episcopus est, qui inter presbyteros primus est Denique Timotheum presbyterum ordinatum significat, sed quia ante se alterum non habebat, episcopus erat "*

After such explicit declarations as those above quoted, from Grotius, it surely must be an attempt which presumes not a little on the reader's credulity or ignorance, to undertake to class that eminent man among the supporters of *Dr C.'s* notions of episcopacy, and not less so

* See Campbell's Lect on Eccl Hist, p 116

[" After the bishop he places the order of deacon. Why? unless it be because the ordination of bishop and presbyter is one? For each is a priest. But the bishop is first, so that every bishop is a presbyter, not every presbyter a bishop For he is a bishop who is first among the presbyters. Finally, he declares that Timothy was ordained a presbyter, but because he had no other before him, he was a bishop "—Ed]

certainly to rank in the same class even *Calvin* and *Beza !* The latter of these eminent men, indeed, according to Grotius, (who was expressly speaking at the same time of "the churches which have no bishops,") thought it ought by no means to be omitted that "it was essential that, by the perpetual ordination of God, it was, it is, and it will be necessary *that some one in the presbytery, chief both in place and dignity, should preside* to govern the proceedings with that right which is given to him by God ·" meaning obviously, that in every presbytery there should be a *presiding presbyter, chief both in place and dignity,* to govern the proceedings *as president,* with a right to exact the submission required by order and the ecclesiastical constitution, in accordance with the general principle ordained of God,—let every soul be subject to the higher powers,—agreeably to the specific constitution of government under which they live, whether of church or state.

In fine, Grotius's view of episcopacy *in fact,* apart from *names* and *forms,* which do not at all alter *things,* is set forth with the lucidness of a sunbeam, in the following emphatic passage :—"And (if with Zanchius [says that very eminent man] I will acknowledge the truth) *in reality* no men were *bishops* more than those very men whose authority availed to oppose even the episcopate."

The above extracts are from Grotius's work on Church Government, in the words of the translations adopted by Dr. C himself

In regard to *Calvin* Dr C makes an extract of some length from his Institutes, [book iv, chap iv, 2,] which I beg leave to submit entire, for a reason which will immediately appear.   It is as follows :—

"They named all those on whom was enjoined the office of teaching presbyters   These chose one of their number in every city, to whom in particular they gave the title of bishop, lest from equality, as usually hap-

pens, dissensions should arise. Yet the bishop was
not so superior in honour and dignity, that he had dominion over his colleagues · but those duties which a
consul performs in the senate, that he may report concerning matters, collect their opinions, go before others
in consulting, admonishing, exhorting, regulate the
whole proceedings by his own authority, and execute
what may have been determined in common council,
that office the bishop sustained in the assembly of presbyters. And the ancients themselves confess that it
was introduced by human agreement, through the necessity of the times Thus Jerome, on the epistle to
Titus, says: 'A presbyter is the same as a bishop.
And before that by the instigation of the devil dissensions were made in religion, and it was said among the
people, I am of Paul, I of Cephas, the churches were
governed by the common council of presbyters Afterward, that the seeds of dissension might be taken away,
the whole charge was committed to one. As, therefore,
the presbyters know that they are subject by the custom of the church to him who is over them, so the
bishops may have known that they are superior to the
presbyters more by custom than by the Lord's appointment, and ought to govern the church in common' He
elsewhere, however, teaches how ancient the institution
was For he says, at Alexandria, from Mark the evangelist to Heraclas and Dionysius, the presbyters always
placed one chosen from themselves in a higher degree,
whom they call bishop."—"To every city was allotted
a certain region which received its presbyters from
thence, and was added to the body of that church —
Every college (as I have said) was subject to one
bishop, for the sake of government only and preserving
peace, who so exceeded others in dignity that he was
subject to the assembly of the brethren But if the
tract of country which was in his bishopric was so
large that he could not fulfil all the duties of a bishop,

presbyters were appointed in certain places through that country who should discharge his duty in minor matters "

In the sentence immediately following this extract, Dr C says : "In this passage Calvin fully admits the main facts contended for by Episcopalians."* He certainly does admit in it the main facts contended for by *Methodist Episcopalians;* and if Dr C. is satisfied with the footing on which *Calvin* places the subject in this passage, then am I perfectly content here to end the controversy, and to leave every reader for himself to judge and interpret Calvin's language without a word of comment from any quarter. For nothing, to my humble apprehension, could be more diametrically opposite to Dr. C's "main" positions, than those here asserted by that learned and eminent reformer.

On the same page with the above extract there is a note of Dr C's, which seems to me to be a curiosity in logic. He undertakes to prove that Jerome "did not then confess it, as Calvin says," "that a presbyter is the same as a bishop" He commences, indeed, with saying, " according to Dr Miller :" but concludes with the broad affirmation which I have just stated. What then did Jerome do ? Why, says Dr. C , "He only inferred, and he himself calls it an opinion" That is to say, Jerome's words, according to Dr Miller, are,—" A presbyter therefore is the same as a bishop "† And yet Dr C gravely and stoutly denies that, even with regard to the primitive period of which Jerome was speaking, this is either a confession or an assertion that a presbyter was the same as a bishop ! With an author who can allow himself such liberty argument surely must be hopeless

To be obliged to read the same things a hundred times over in one small volume is irksome enough ; but

---

* Page 198   † Miller's Letters, p. 180.

to be obliged to answer them as often would be still more so , and yet one must do this, or pass by much that Dr. C. says. The very strong terms and phrases " impossible," " utterly impossible," " the only possibility," " the very idea is absurd," " an absurdity too great to be advocated by any man in his senses," and others similar, which so frequently occur in this gentleman's production, seem to me neither to add any special grace to style, nor force to argument, and to evince rather more of overweening conceit of his own opinions on the part of the author, than of modest respect for his readers, who—as above said—within the vast scope of bare possibility, might possibly happen to differ from him

For example, Dr. C. says, " The only possibility of a breach in the episcopal succession could arise from the bishops at some period of the church laying aside the ceremony of ordination, or allowing other than bishops to ordain bishops The first idea is an absurdity too great to be advocated by any man in his senses , and as to the other, when no instance can be produced by the ablest and most learned advocates for presbyterian ordination, in which presbyters laid on hands by permission of the church until the year 657—."*

Now in regard to "the first idea" in the above passage, I would just remind Dr C of "the case of the episcopal churches in the United States" at the close of our revolutionary war , and then let him consider the " Sketch of a Frame of Government," offered by Dr. White on that occasion, in which he says,—" ' In each smaller district there should be elected a general vestry or convention, consisting of a convenient number, (the minister to be one) They should elect a clergyman their *permanent president ,* who, in conjunction with other

---

* Page 206. Dr C afterward, page 210, acknowledges this date to be erroneous, and that what he alludes to here was in the fourth century, and not in the seventh, as here

clergymen, to be also appointed by the body, may exer
cise such powers as are purely spiritual, *particularly that
of admitting to the ministry,*' p 11."

" Again · 'The conduct meant to be recommended is,
to include in the proposed frame of government a *general approbation of episcopacy* and a declaration of an
intention to procure the succession as soon as conve-
niently may be ; but in the meantime *to carry the plan
into effect without waiting for the succession*' Ibid , p 15."

" ' But it will also be said,' continues Dr. White,
' that the very name of *" bishop"* is offensive ; if so,
change it for another ; let the *superior clergyman* be a
president, a *superintendent,* or in plain English, and according to the literal translation of the original, an
overseer. However, if *names* are to be reprobated, because the powers annexed to them are abused, there are
few appropriated to either civil or ecclesiastical distinctions, which would retain their places in our catalogue.'
Ibid., p 17 "

Is it not plain from the above that Dr W. did not
consider it so perfectly absurd an idea that there might
be a valid episcopacy in fact, under whatever name,
simply by election, without the usual ceremony of ordination ? It would seem, he must either have meant this,
or that there should be an episcopal consecration by
presbyters Dr C may take his choice

Again : some very learned men have been of opinion,
(and I merely mention this in evidence that the idea
possibly may not be so utterly absurd,) that the episcopal church of Alexandria did perhaps actually dispense
with the usual form of imposing hands in the creation of
bishops, for about two hundred years , using no other
forms than simple election, and the subsequent instalment and salutation, as the army created an emperor,
or deacons an archdeacon

As to the other part of Dr C 's alternative, viz , "allowing other than bishops [in his sense] to ordain

bishops,"—he cannot be permitted, without contradiction, to persist in repeating a hundred times over, when at least the long series of such ordinations, virtually or formally, in the ancient apostolical church of Alexandria stands recorded, in so many learned pages, an imperishable refutation of the baseless assertion.   Nor is there any evidence that "the church," universal or particular, ever condemned them   As to "the ancient church" of the fourth and fifth centuries, and the councils of that period, they have already been sufficiently considered *

The progressive tendency, as the church became more and more corrupt, and the hierarchy more firmly established, to restrict the right of ordaining bishops, is manifest from the fact, admitted by Dr. C.,† that after the rise of metropolitan bishops, they began gradually to claim to themselves this exclusive right

Before closing his work, Dr C says, "It has been doubted whether the ordination of Archbishop Parker, through whom all the bishops of the Protestant Episcopal Church of England derive their ordination, was perfectly canonical ; because the persons who ordained him had been deprived of their bishoprics and expelled the country by the Popish party, on the accession of Mary to the crown of England   The question to be settled in this case is, whether a bishop who is expelled from his bishopric by a successful party, in the contest about doctrines which have in all ages agitated the church, is hereby deprived of his *character* of bishop."‡

On this quotation I would ask, (1) Was the contest of the English reformers with the Church of Rome one merely " about doctrines ?"—Why, then, was that peti-

---

* Dr Jortin remarks, that " he who will believe all that he finds related by the writers of the fourth and fifth centuries, should be provided with a double portion of credulity, and have the stomach of an ostrich to digest fables "—*Remarks on Eccl Hist* , vol 1, p. 168

† Page 207.   ‡ Ibid

tion inserted in the early litany of the Church of England, "From the tyranny of the bishop of Rome, and all his detestable enormities, good Lord, deliver us?"

(2) What does Dr C. mean by the episcopal "*character?*" That he does not mean the personal religious or moral character of a bishop is plain. Does he mean, then, that mysterious something which Romanists assert to be imprinted in orders, and which some of them define to be "a power to work a spiritual effect?" or, with others of them, does he admit "the *character*" to be merely "a deputation to a special office?"* Whether, even according to the former definition, the *character* may not be lost or taken away, I shall not here discuss † But if Dr C. intends it in the

---

* The reader may see some curious disquisitions on this subject in Sarpi's History of the Council of Trent, page 593. In the debate in that body on the question of the *character*, was involved the fundamental point in this controversy, viz, whether in the sacrament of *orders*, as the Romanists consider it, any higher *character* can be imprinted than that of *priesthood* On this point, even at that period, late in the sixteenth century, the doctors and theologues, prelates, and cardinals, in that famous papal assembly itself, were greatly divided

† The reader who desires to know the true "character" of those who filled the "apostolical chairs," both in the eastern and western churches, during a long series of the boasted successions, *by divine right*, from which high-church ultraists, Greek or Roman, Protestant or Papal, claim exclusive title to minister in holy things, may see it amply and revoltingly enough portrayed in Mosheim's Ecclesiastical History, vol. ii, pp. 389, 390. The following is a specimen —

"To those who consider the primitive dignity, and the solemn nature of the ministerial character, the corruptions of the clergy must appear deplorable beyond all expression These corruptions were mounted to the most enormous height in that dismal period of the church which we have now before us Both in the eastern and western provinces, the clergy were, for the most part, shamefully illiterate and stupid, ignorant more especially in religious matters, equally enslaved to sensuality and superstition, and capable of the most abominable and flagitious deeds This miserable degeneracy of the sacred order was, according to the most credible accounts, principally owing to the pretended chiefs and rulers of the universal church, who indulged themselves in the commission of the most odious crimes, and abandoned themselves to the lawless impulse of the most licentious passions without reluctance or remorse, who confounded, in short, all difference between just and unjust, to satisfy their impious ambition, and whose spiritual empire was such a diversified scene of iniquity and violence as never was

latter sense, then may it not be lost by deprivation, as in the case of the Protestant bishops, of whom Dr. C speaks, in the reign of Mary, who were deprived by the existing authority, both ecclesiastical and civil? The case of the bishop of Worcester, who fled to the continent on the death of Mary, and was recognised as a bishop in the Council of Trent, is not parallel. For in the latter case it was the papal church acknowledging its own bishop; whereas, the former was that of bishops resisting and separating from that mother church from which they had derived their authority, and to which they had owed obedience, and who, consequently, were *schismatics*, both on [Dr C's] principles and those of the Church of Rome

Dr. Miller quotes a passage from *Hilary*, a Roman deacon in the fourth century, which he renders thus — "In *Egypt*, even at this day, the presbyters ordain in the bishop's absence" No, says Dr C, the passage does not mean that they ordain, but that they confirm, the word used by Hilary is "*consignant*," which Ainsworth renders "*seal, sign, mark, register, record, confirm, and ratify.*" Now, continues Dr. C., "there is not one of these words that does not correspond with the real

exhibited under any of those temporal tyrants who have been the scourges of mankind We may form some notion of the Grecian patriarchs from the single example of Theophylact, who, according to the testimonies of the most respectable writers, made the most impious traffic of ecclesiastical promotions, and expressed no sort of care about any thing but his dogs and horses Degenerate, however, and licentious as these patriarchs might be, they were, generally speaking, less profligate and indecent than the Roman pontifls

"'The history of the Roman pontifls, that lived in this century, is a history of so many monsters, and not of men, and exhibits a horrible series of the most flagitious, tremendous, and complicated crimes, as all writers, even those of the Romish communion, unanimously confess"

Can the most veteran and indomitable controvertist have the hardihood seriously to undertake to persuade Protestant Christians of the 19th century, that the horrible "monsters" above mentioned, in both the eastern and western hemisphere, were truly "called of God, as was Aaron,"—"moved by the Holy Ghost," and throughout their flagitious career enjoyed exclusively the fulfilment of that gracious promise, "Lo, I am with you alway?" He who can digest such a fable, must indeed, as Jortin said on another occasion, "have the stomach of an ostrich."

signification of *confirming* by the bishop —But there is not one of these words that has any reference to setting apart by ordination "* The reader will not forget that Dr. C elsewhere denies as stoutly that presbyters anciently confirmed as that they ordained. Here he is obliged to admit it to be Hilary's testimony that they confirmed, in order to avoid admitting it as a testimony that they ordained But then what becomes of the "*character*" imprinted in ordination , if not one of the words used by Ainsworth to express the sense of *consigno* "has any reference to setting apart by ordination?" To "sign," to "mark,"—have these terms no reference whatever to impressing or imprinting a "*character?*"

But there is much more yet to be said as to the ground on which the regularity of the archiepiscopal ordination of Dr Parker, through whom all the bishops of the Protestant Episcopal Church of England and America claim title, is disputed In the reign of Henry VIII the bishops of the Popish party,—although it does not appear that Cranmer (or perhaps the rest) did so, *in that reign*, as Burnet says,—took out commissions, by which they solemnly acknowledged "That all jurisdiction, civil and ecclesiastical, flowed from the king, and that they exercised it only at the king's courtesie ; and as they had of his bounty, so they would be ready to deliver it up when he should be pleased to call for it, and therefore the king did empower them, *in his stead*, to ordain, give institution, and do all the other parts of the episcopal function, which was to last during his pleasure."† "By this [says Bishop Burnet expressly] they were made indeed *the king's bishops*"‡

Again ·—In the succeeding reign of Edward VI, in the year 1547, the same historian says, "All that held

* Page 125.
† Burnet's Abridgment of the History of the Reformation, book i, pp 228, 229
‡ Ibid . p 229.

offices were required to come and renew their commissions, and to swear allegiance to the king among the rest, the bishops came and took out *such commissions as were granted in the former reign*, only by those they were subaltern to the king's vicegerent, but there being none now in that office they were immediately subaltern to the king ; and by them they were to hold their bishoprics only during the king's pleasure, and were impowered in the king's name, as his delegates, to perform all the parts of the episcopal function *Cranmer* set an example to the rest in taking out one of those. It was thought fit thus to keep the bishops under the terror of such an arbitrary power lodged in the king, that so it might be more easy to turn them out, if they should much oppose what might be done in points of religion: but the ill consequences of such an unlimited power being well foreseen, the bishops that were afterward promoted were not so fettered, but were provided to hold their bishoprics during life.' *

In the same reign an act of parliament was passed, "that the *conge d'elire* and the election pursuant to it being but a shadow, since the person was named by the king, should cease for the future, and that bishops should be named by the king's letters patent, and thereupon be consecrated "†

" The form of the patent was, That the king appointed such a one to be bishop during his natural life, or as long as he behaved himself well ; and gave him power to ordain or deprive ministers, to exercise ecclesiastical jurisdiction, and perform all the other parts of the episcopal function that by the word of God were committed to bishops, and this they were to do *in the king's name* and *by his authority* "‡

Among those created bishops by the king's letters patent, by which he was empowered to ordain, and to

---

* Burnet's Abridgment of the History of the Reformation, book ii, pp 4, 5.
† Ib., p 37   ‡ Ib., p. 193.

perform all the other parts of the *episcopal* function, *in the king's name* and *by his authority*, was Barlow, one of those very persons by whom Dr. Parker was set apart for the office of archbishop.* Another of them was Scory, and Neal calls Barlow and Scory bishops elect "† He states also, that although *Coverdale* and *Hodgkins*, the remaining two, assisted in Parker's ordination, yet they never exercised the episcopal character afterward ‡ It is certain, moreover, that efforts were made, *in the first instance*, to induce *three of the Popish bishops who had not been deprived* in the preceding reign to unite in the ordination, and they were first named (viz *Tonstal, Bourn,* and *Pool*) in the warrant which was issued by the queen (Elizabeth) for this purpose   This is a demonstration that the union of three bishops who had not been deprived was then deemed important, if not essential, to the canonical validity of the ordination: otherwise, the warrant, in the circumstances of that time, would never have embraced three Popish bishops. But not one of the bishops who had not been deprived would act   And hence the ordination, from necessity, not of choice, was performed by deprived bishops

In this state of facts then the objection to the canonical validity of Dr Parker's archiepiscopal ordination is, that it was performed by persons who had been legally deprived in the preceding reign, and had not been restored   About seven years afterward, indeed, the matter was brought before the British parliament, both houses of which, to silence clamor, confirmed the ordination of Parker, and the ordinations derived from him   But be it remembered, (1,) that this only proves the more strongly the seriousness of the doubts then existing as to the validity of what had been done , and, (2,) that the confirmation of it *by an act of parliament* was, after all, but a *lay* confirmation

* Burnet's Hist , &c., p. 193
† History of the Puritans, vol i, p. 181.   ‡ Ibid.

10*

Yet farther —In another part of his work, p. 149, Dr C argues that the consent or intention of the grantor is necessary to the validity of a grant, and builds a similar argument on the understanding of the grantee, at the time of receiving the grant   Now I have proved that in the year 1547 the English bishops took out episcopal commissions as " subaltern to the king," and to perform all the parts of the episcopal function *in his name*, and *as his delegates*.*   On these terms, then, episcopal authority was both granted and received, and it was so expressly *understood* and *agreed* by *both parties* at the time.   The Protestant bishops among these were deprived in the succeeding reign; and when they took part, in the year 1559, in the ordination of Parker, had never been legally restored.   This I believe to be the true state of the case, and shall submit it to the reader's own judgment whether, on the principles by which the deprived bishops held their commissions, and those laid down by Dr. C. as above quoted, the episcopal ordination of Dr Parker was clearly and perfectly canonical and valid

* Burnet, Book II, pp 4, 5.

[*Unfinished Remarks on Bishop Onderdonk's tract, entitled*
"Episcopacy tested by Scripture"]

In passing to Dr. Onderdonk's tract, the first remark
I have to make is, that it is essentially defective in not
furnishing at the outset a clear definition of the precise
import which he attaches to the term "episcopacy" The
manner in which he evidently avails himself of the vague-
ness of this term throughout his tract renders his whole
argument fallacious, and a mere sophism.   The *ground*
on which he proposes to build his argument is otherwise excellent, and exactly that on which we desire to
meet all opponents; viz, "the Scriptural evidence of
episcopacy." Equally excellent is the principle by
which he agrees that the discussion ought to be restricted,
viz, that "no argument is worth taking into account that
has not a palpable bearing on the clear and naked topic,
—the Scriptural evidence." I regret exceedingly, therefore, that it did not occur to Dr O , or else that he did
not find it convenient, or think it expedient, or even necessary in order to a fair issue, to state with candour
and precision what he means by a term of such fundamental importance in the discussion as to involve within
itself, it would seem, some one specific frame of polity,
of universal and perpetual obligation, by Divine authority, on the whole church of Christ on earth   This
capital defect at the very commencement of Dr. O.'s
offer of an issue in the argument is the more to be re-
gretted, because he undoubtedly knows, not only that
the term "episcopacy" is a very vague one in itself,
but that it is very variously understood, not only by different denominations of Christians, but by different
classes of the same denomination, and even within his
own   The Romanists have an " episcopacy ;" the
Church of England, and the Protestant Episcopal, and
some others, an "episcopacy ," and high and low church

Episcopalians among themselves; the Methodist Episcopal have an "episcopacy;" nay, Presbyterians admit and contend for "episcopacy" And I know not, indeed, any denomination that, in some form and to some extent or other, does not both recognise the principle and practise the thing, viz. some species of ministerial superiority,—graduated or otherwise,—in a superintending care, charge, government, inspection, or oversight of a church or churches

It seems to me, therefore, with great deference, that it is Dr O himself who inflicts the "forensic injustice" of complicating this "plain topic," by making up an issue so perfectly vague and indefinite that it may be widened or narrowed, stretched or shortened at convenience, as circumstances dictate,—to mean, in fact, almost just any thing or nothing

If by "episcopacy" be meant that high-church scheme of ecclesiastical polity which maintains that there are three, and only three, essentially distinct ministerial orders, divinely ordained to be universally and perpetually binding on the church of Christ, so that without them there can be no true church or valid Christian ministry or ordinances, and that of these three orders the episcopal, as inherently and essentially distinct and supreme by Divine appointment and right, has alone and exclusively the power and authority to ordain other ministers,—and that all this is apparent from God's own word, as an essential part of the Christian revelation :—then we understand the issue, and are prepared to meet it.

I must here, however, do Dr. O the justice to say, and I do it with pleasure, that from *this* issue *he*, at least, blenches; and in so doing, as I humbly conceive, he clearly gives up the essence of the high-church cause, and confesses it to be untenable It ought not to be forgotten, moreover, that this respectable prelate, the "assistant bishop of the Protestant Episcopal Church in the commonwealth of Pennsylvania," wrote *after* Dr C, with his book before him, and probably understood the subject at least as well as the medical gentleman just named, and was evidently as much disposed to press the high-church pretensions to as great an extent as he conscientiously could. Yet this more candid, more liberal, or better informed opponent, with all his manifest predisposition and bias to the other side, felt himself bound to say that those who "maintain that episcopacy is essential to the being of a church," assert an "extreme opinion," to which he "subscribes not."*

Inconsistent, however, as Dr. O. is, in admitting that episcopacy, in his sense of it, is not essential to the being of a church, and yet maintaining that "*no* plea," not even that of "necessity," will justify a departure from it,—I shall proceed with an examination of the process by which he reaches his conclusions. And in doing so, I must give notice, once for all, that in speaking of episcopacy as advocated by him, I do it always in the high-church sense, with the single exception above named, as to its indispensableness to the being of a church.

Another fatal fallacy which lurks at the very foundation of Dr O's argument is the indefinite phrase under cover of which he would introduce the absolutely *imperative* character of episcopacy as a duty of moral obligation, in obedience to a Divine ordinance. "If episcopacy [he says] be set forth in Scripture, it is the ordinance of God; and the citizens professing Christianity are individually bound to conform to it"†

If it be "*set forth*" in Scripture! How convenient a phrase! and why used? Why not say plainly, If it be *commanded* in Scripture? Obviously, because it is well

---

* Page 5   [A note in the MS here indicates that the author intended to insert something corresponding to what may be found on p 10 —Ed.]
† Page 4.

known that it is not so. And why then should we labour and exert even the utmost ingenuity of sophistry itself to make the commandment broader than it is? Is it not, as it stands, "exceeding broad,"—exactly as it should be, having neither redundancy nor defect? Who then hath required it at *our* hands to add to it, and to narrow the very covenant mercies of the Father of mercies? May there not be danger on this side as well as on the other? And where, at least, there is so much doubtfulness and difference of opinion among confessedly wise and good men, as to either extreme, is not a medium, as before said, the more probable and safer ground?

The very subtile (I say not subtle) and almost imperceptible manner in which Dr O would lead his readers, step by step, through the gradations of his argument, from the slenderest premises, is indeed worthy of the "forensic" ingenuity of a special pleader. At a subsequent stage, he takes the ground, *interrogatively*, that "a mere *hint* or *intimation* contained in Scripture, (always excepting what refers to things or circumstances declared to be transient, or such in their nature,) though it have not the force of an express command, is—*sufficiently* binding on every servant of God "* And although at one time he distinctly disallows "that episcopal claims *unchurch* all non-episcopal denominations," and admits that such may be worthy professors of the true religion, accepted of God through the Saviour, and not only not inferior to " *the church*," but even superior to it in both moral and spiritual character, yet in the very next paragraph he assumes that those same " episcopal claims" can be sufficiently proved from Scripture, to make their rejection " *a clear contravention of the word of God*," pp. 6, 7. Now, in the first place, it is denied that there is even any " hint or intimation" in Scripture

* Page 10.

that it is " the Divine will" that high-church episcopacy should be, universally and perpetually, the morally obligatory constitution of all Christian churches And it is affirmed, on the other hand, that there are very many hints and intimations from which the contrary may be most fairly inferred And, in the second place, the very resort to mere hints and intimations, by a disputant of such ability, and so well read in Scripture, seems a sufficient indication that he was himself conscious of the extreme scantiness of any better Scripture proofs, and consequently of the extreme questionableness and narrowness, to say the least, of the foundation on which he would rear his weighty fabric.

In regard to Dr O 's illustrations of Scripture hints or illustrations, his interpretation of some is denied, and the appositeness and force of others.   He says, for example,—" St Paul says of the Gentiles, ' These, having not the law, are a law unto themselves :' they had not the positive revealed law, yet the light of nature, which only intimates what we ought to do, but does not specifically prescribe it, was ' a law' to them, having sufficient obligation to make its suggestions their duty, and to give those suggestions full authority in ' their conscience ' and surely the hints recorded by the DEITY in his word are not inferior in obligation to those afforded in his works."*

Now (1,) by "the law" which the Gentiles had not, Rom. ii, 14, St. Paul evidently meant *the written law*, as contained in the Old Testament, and (2,) he says no such thing as that " the light of nature" " afforded in his works'—the works of Deity—" intimates what we ought to do," or " was a law to them,"—the Gentiles,—" having sufficient obligation to make its suggestions their duty, and to give those suggestions *full authority* in their conscience." We deny this whole doctrine. And St Paul

* Page 10.

plainly shows that he meant no such thing, by adding immediately in the next verse, "which show the work of the law *written in their hearts*"—by the very same hand, doubtless,—for what other hand could do it,—which engraved the commandments on the tables of stone. This was to them, then, *a positive Divine law*,—their authoritative rule of action and of judgment, which they could not slight or violate and be guiltless, or " accepted with God "

As an illustration of his position, Dr. O. says :— " There is no record of a command to observe a Sabbath during the whole antediluvian and patriarchal ages, will it then be alleged that the mere declaration that GOD 'blessed and sanctified the seventh day' did not sufficiently *imply* that it was the Divine will that the seventh day should be kept holy ?"*

Does Dr. O seriously intend to say, then, that the sanctity of the Sabbath as a Divine institution is not *expressly* contained in the very words of the institution as recorded by the inspired historian? The original Hebrew word קדש, rendered in our version *sanctified*, (literally, *made holy*,) in the Septuagint is ἡγίασεν. (of the same import) Buxtorf,—" sacrari, consecrari, sanctificari, sanctum, sacrum esse vel fieri " Leigh's Critica Sacra,—" Ab usu communi ad divinum separatus, consecratus," &c And by Parkhurst (on this place)— " *To set apart, separate, or appropriate to sacred or religious purposes, to sanctify, to consecrate.*"

His second example is from " the rite of sacrifice," respecting which he asks whether " the record of the example of Abel in the antediluvian age, and of those of Noah, Abraham, &c, afterward, were not sufficient *intimations* from God that to offer this sacramental atonement was a duty " The answer to this is, (1,) That without a direct revelation from God of his will in this

* Page 10

respect, there is no reason to believe that the idea of offering animals in sacrifice as a sacramental atonement would ever have entered into the mind of man, or have been his duty. and, (2,) that in the cases of Abel and Noah, the Divine pleasure in this specific, definite thing was explicitly signified and, (3,) that in the case of Abram it was *explicitly commanded*, see Gen xv, 9, &c , and the command contained an epitome of that very law of sacrifices afterward more fully revealed through Moses

His third example is from the creation, for each other, of one man and one woman ; and it is asked if this be not a sufficient intimation that polygamy is contrary to the will of God With our *present* light this would seem so And yet this is an unfortunate example for Dr O 's theory For how does he reconcile it with the *practice* of polygamy by some of those who, under that dispensation, stood highest, nevertheless, in the Divine favour?

His fourth is, that " there is no positive command for infant baptism," and yet a sufficiency, " whether as examples or as intimations," to authorize it In all the arguments for infant baptism we agree, and urge them for the conviction of others But we think it is also positively commanded, at least as positively as female communion. The command is to disciple all nations, which Dr O , it is presumed, will agree to be the true import of the original, Matt. xxviii, 19. And as children are a part of all nations, and may be discipled, they are as clearly embraced in the command as females are in reference to the communion under the term man. And, corresponding with this is the express promise annexed to the ordinance,—" For the promise is to you and to your children," Acts ii, 39 · a term embracing their posterity certainly,—but as certainly, in our estimation, their offspring then living

His fifth is in regard to the change of the day of rest and devotion, from the seventh to the first Does he mean to say, then, that the moral obligation consists in the observance of the first day specifically, or of a seventh part of time · in other words, is he of opinion that there are sufficient *hints* in Scripture to constitute the former a Christian law of universal and perpetual obligation, the neglect of which would be sinful, even where the latter,—the seventh day for example,—the laws of any country allowing it, should be sacredly and conscientiously observed ?

But if Dr O 's rule be a good one, it ought to admit of being carried through and if it be found to prove too much, it must be allowed to be good for nothing The objection that monarchy is "set forth" in Scripture, as well as episcopacy, he has answered in a note, pp 43, 44   But some of the very points made in that answer justify, I think, some other objections, to which I do not perceive how that answer, or any other on his principles, can satisfactorily be applied   He says, for example, that monarchy, being an ordinance of man, might be changed by man; and when the objector urges farther that the Deity himself gave a king to Israel, he answers that it was "in anger."   Suppose then we take (1,) the case of a national church—a national ecclesiastical establishment , and, (2,) a corresponding establishment by law of the system of *tithes*.   Such, indisputably, were the institutions which Jehovah ordained for his ancient church and people,—and certainly not in anger   And high churchmen, moreover, and Dr C. especially, very strenuously and boldly insist upon it that "what Aaron and his sons were, bishops and priests now are "   If this analogy be a correct one, is it not a pretty strong "intimation" of what ought to follow, and the "hint" that a national establishment and tithes are, agreeable to the Divine will, as clearly "set forth" in Scripture as some others of Dr O 's "examples?" In one of his notes, p 44, he says —" It has been said that the appointment of a king for *Israel* by the Deity,

is an intimation of the Divine will in favour of royal government, and that therefore that form of civil magis-
tracy must be as binding as episcopacy. We reply, (he
continues,) that if such an intimation of the Divine will
existed, it would unquestionably be binding on Christians." He then proceeds to show that this was not the
fact, because a king was given to them "in anger," in
consequence of their perverseness and ambition in insisting on having one   But this reasoning does not at
all apply to the national church establishment and tithes,
which, according to Dr O.'s doctrine of intimations and
his reasoning upon it, must be binding on Christians,
and, consequently, conformity to these intimations cannot be refused, in nations professing Christianity, "*in
foro conscientiæ, animoque integro*"

Again   Was it not sufficiently intimated under the
Levitical economy, that priests ought not to enter the
service of the sanctuary till thirty years of age, and that
they ought to be discharged at fifty? Did not our Lord
give an example in his own case of not entering on the
work of the ministry till thirty years of age ; and of
washing the disciples' feet? Is there not a sufficient intimation of the Divine approbation of the community of
goods in the first Christian church   and in choosing an
apostle by *lot* · Paul's circumcising Timothy   the taking
of illiterate men from the common occupations of life for
apostles and ministers?

Other examples might be adduced, but for the present
I shall rest this part of the cause with these

In order to prove the duty of obedience to wicked and
worthless priests and bishops, Dr O. alleges that saying
of our Lord, "The scribes and Pharisees sit in Moses'
seat," &c, Matt xxiii, 2   It should be observed, however, (1,) That our Lord simply states the fact, "they
sit," &c , or rather, they "sat," for in the Greek the
verb is in the past tense.   (2,) That they occupied that
seat by national authority , and so far obedience was due

to them as a national constitution, and as readers of the
law and of the prophets. But that he did not mean to
say that those wicked men among them who then occupied it, did so by Divine appointment or with the Divine
approbation, or that the people were bound to render
them unlimited obedience, is manifest from his own
heavy denunciation of them in that same chapter, and
elsewhere, as a very generation of vipers, charging them
with even making void the law of God through their
traditions and teaching, that they shut up the kingdom
of heaven against men, and made their proselytes even
doubly more the children of hell than themselves If,
therefore, Dr O. could ever allege Scripture for the mere
fact that "bishops," whether by national law, usage, or
usurpation, "sit in the apostles' seats" still, if they be
such a generation as those scribes and Pharisees were,
making their proselytes even doubly more the children of hell than themselves, and making void the law,
&c., we should say that they ought to be denounced as
our Lord denounced those whited sepulchres of that day,
and the people taught to beware of them, and placed as
soon as practicable under the guidance of better teachers
than those "fools and blind," however learned, &c But
Dr. O. produces no such scripture as that "bishops sit
in the apostles' seats "* And for such a "claim"—a
claim which asserts for bishops, however wicked and
worthless, erroneous in doctrine, and fatally corrupting
in morals—the place of infallible guides, as the apostles
were, to whom universal, perpetual, implicit obedience
is due, no authority short of a direct and positive "thus
saith the Lord," can be allowed ; nor, indeed, does such
a thing seem possible, without imputing sin and contradiction to the Deity himself.

As to Balaam, although he prophesied the truth,
though himself "a wicked man," yet Dr O certainly

* Page 5

knows who hath said, " *Many* will say to me in that day, Lord, Lord, have we not prophesied in thy name, &c., and then will I profess unto them, *I never knew you;* depart from me," &c , I never appointed, approved, nor acknowledged you as mine

In regard to the farther plea for the obligation on the people to continue in subjection to wicked priests, and in communion with wicked churches, from the fact that "the sons of Eli, bad as they were, ceased not to be priests," and that "the Israelites at large were often corrupt and idolatrous," yet "never lost their standing as the earthly and visible church, till their dispensation was superseded by that of the Gospel,"* there are two answers the first is, that the Jewish institution was of a mixed character, being national and political, as well as ecclesiastical, and the priests were such by *hereditary descent,* which Dr. O. might just as well allege as a sufficient intimation that it ought to be so still But the Christian dispensation, being designed for the whole race of man, and to be perpetual, is wholly spiritual, having no connection with any political or national establishment whatever "My kingdom," said its Founder emphatically, "is not of this world," and hence the polity of a Jewish politico-ecclesiastical institution, and the precedents *tolerated* under it, have no binding force whatever, since that dispensation has been totally abolished, and *is* now "superseded" by another, wholly pure and spiritual

The second answer is, that Dr. O 's argument would have been an admirable one for the papal hierarchy at the era of the Reformation, and if it be a just and conclusive one, demonstrates that the Church of England and the Protestant Episcopal Church in this country are *schismatical,* and ought to have continued in communion with " *the Church*" which then was, though all its priests

* Page 5

should even have been as bad as the sons of Eli, and the Church "at large," like the priests, "corrupt," and even "idolatrous" such seems to me to be the inevitable consequence of Dr O s argument, if a good one , that therefore the champions of Rome ought not to have been "worsted by the extraneous argument" of the glorious reformers, founded on the corruptions, the oppressions, the false doctrines, (like those of the scribes and Pharisees who sat in Moses' seat, making void the commandments of God by their tradition and teaching,) or even the idolatrous character of the Church at large, and the "detestable enormities of its bishops and priests" The argument certainly proves too much for the *Protestant* cause, and, if a conclusive one, ought manifestly to drive us all back to "the Church' from which our predecessors so wickedly separated.

In proceeding to the second department of his essay, "an exhibition of the *Scriptural evidence* relating to this controversy," Dr O professes to "begin by stating the precise point at issue" This, he says, is "between two systems only, episcopacy, and parity, or the Presbyterian ministry :"* and by "parity," he states that he means that system which "declares that there is but one order" of men authorized to minister in sacred things. We beg leave to repeat, therefore, that between high church and *us*, this is not the issue There is a third or middle system, which is that of the Methodist Episcopal polity This system not only admits but maintains the doctrine of *two orders*, strictly considered, and a third *degree*, or *grade*, officially superior in executive authority and jurisdiction to the body of presbyters out of which and by which it is constituted To this *officially* superior order, in a more general sense of this term, is committed, according to this system, also the exclusive and actual authority to ordain, the general supervision, whether in a smaller or larger diocese, and

* Page 11.

the chief administration of spiritual discipline, besides enjoying all the powers of the other grades   Yet one cannot go so far with Dr O. as to say, " If we cannot authenticate the claims of the episcopal office, we will surrender those of our deacons, and let all power be confined to the one office of presbyters *"

So far as *we* are concerned, then, Dr O 's statement of the issue is a mere begging of the question.   The true issue between him and *us* is, Is ordination by presbyters in any exigence and under any and all circumstances, wholly incompatible with episcopacy, *in the Scriptural sense* of that *term* or *thing*, and in itself, by God's word, unlawful and void?   The affirmative of this question is what Dr O has to sustain, if his argument is to have any bearing on us ; and, in this view of it, I proceed to an examination of his scripture proofs

It is proper here to premise, however, and I beg the reader to bear it in mind, that as Dr O distinctly admits that there may be true Christian churches without episcopacy, it follows necessarily either that episcopacy is not essential to the validity of ordination to the ministry, or that there may be true Christian churches, (and if some, why not all,) *without any ministers at all*   An argument so incongruous must have some flaw, however ingeniously it may be concealed.

At the outset of this "second department" of his essay, Dr O frankly concedes that the name "bishop," in Scripture, is given to presbyters, and that " all that we read in the New Testament concerning ' bishops,' (including of course the words ' overseers' and ' oversight,' which have the same derivation,) is to be regarded as pertaining to that grade," viz , the order of presbyters   " The highest grade he [continues] is there found in those called 'apostles,' and in some other individuals, as Titus, Timothy, and the angels of the seven churches in Asia

* Page 11 —A note in the MS. indicates that it was intended here also to insert from page 10, *ante.*

Minor, who have no official designation given them. It was after the apostolic age [he adds] that the name 'bishop' was taken from the second order and appropriated to the first, as we learn from Theodoret, one of the fathers "*

How is this? After such a preliminary flourish of trumpets, long and loud, about going into *Scripture alone* with the naked question, freed from all extraneous considerations, and exclusively of all other sources of authority or argument, we find ourselves, at the very start, referred to " *Theodoret*, one of the fathers !" What fathers ? Peter we know, and Paul we know ; but in this issue, as offered by Dr O himself, who is Theodoret? Whatever he may be elsewhere, he is an intruder here, and cannot be suffered to say one word, good or bad, on either side.

In his note on the same place, Dr. O. refers to " Videlius" also, in support of the same position. We protest against his admission also, whether he be episcopal or non-episcopal. We demand a clear field , the field chosen, proposed by Dr O himself—the Scripture alone and if he find not there sufficient for his purpose, without aid, direct or incidental, from any other quarter whatever, his only alternative is to give up the contest   The very fact of his flying off to such " extraneous aid," is sufficient indication that he was sensible of the difficulty, if not the impossibility, of connecting his chain without it   He must assume something, or go *out of Scripture*, or inevitably fail, as we believe, to make out his case

This course on the part of Dr. O is the more surprising, as he himself had previously said of certain uninspired authorities referred to, " We reject, therefore, this whole extraneous appendage of the controversy before us ;" and then adds, "that the rule applies to the *fathers*, as much as to later ornaments of the church "†   Is it

* Page 12.   † Pages 8, 9

11

not passing strange, then, that within a few pages afterward, he should himself attempt to avail himself of the authority of one of those very fathers—nay, a father of the *fifth* century, and a *prelate* too!

No evidence then of any thing that was "taken from" the order of presbyters, "after the apostolic age," whether in name or otherwise, can be admitted in the argument before us This would be to travel out of the Scripture record , and by that record alone this cause must be tried.

Again . Within a few sentences afterward, Dr O. says, "The original meaning of bishop was only a presbyter, but the name passed from that middle grade to the highest "* Here again we must stop him, unpleasant and inconvenient as it may be.   There is no such evidence in the record, and he *must not travel out of it.* His assumption, or mere gratuitous assertion, (for the statement amounts to nothing more) can no more be allowed, under this issue, than the evidence of Theodoret.

The *name* "bishop," then, being given up by Dr. O. as meaning, in Scripture, no higher order than presbyter, his next resort is, to see "if we can find the *thing* sought, i e , an office higher than that of presbyters or elders."†

If this be "the thing sought," there neither is nor can be any controversy on the subject. That there are in the New Testament higher offices mentioned than that of mere presbyters or bishops, I presume no one can think of questioning But, unfortunately for Dr O.'s system, his argument again proves too much If one higher office can be proved by it, most assuredly several can ; and consequently, on this basis, more than three orders must necessarily be admitted. For example, to repeat a passage above quoted from Dr O., in which he says, "the highest grade is there found [in the New

* Page 12.   † Ibid

11*

Testament] in those called apostles, *and in some other individuals*, as Titus, Timothy," &c Now (to say nothing at present of the angels of the Asiatic churches, about whom the Scriptures give us so little information) does any unsophisticated reader of the New Testament, who has no system or purposes of party to serve, believe that any " other individuals" exercised the same office that the apostles did? Rejecting all regard to mere *names*, and looking at *things* and *facts*, can any thing be plainer than that the offices of Titus and Timothy, for instance, (as Dr O names these particularly) were inferior to that of Paul? Thus much on this point here, by the way. It will be resumed hereafter

In another place, Dr O says of the word " bishop," " In Scripture, it means a presbyter, properly so called; out of Scripture, according to the usage next to universal of all ages since the sacred canon was closed, it means"*—Dear sir, you must be pleased to excuse us for interrupting you so frequently—no " usage," any more than other testimony " out of Scripture" has any place here, and you cannot be allowed to introduce it: you yourself have given the challenge to test this question by *Scripture alone*, and to that you must confine yourself, or acknowledge yourself " worsted "

As to the " fact of the existence of episcopacy" in Scripture,—that is to say, that there was, in the apostolical age, an official oversight both of churches and ministers, with *us* there is no dispute We admit, and maintain, as fully as Dr O does or can, that the apostles, in common, did exercise such an oversight—an itinerant general superintendency over the whole church, which was an itinerant general episcopacy in *fact;* and that others under them did exercise a subordinate oversight by their appointment and direction; this we grant with all readiness and pleasure, as we shall do whatever *does* appear in the Scripture, lead us

* Page 12

where it may   We agree, moreover, that it is a fair inference from this fact, that an official itinerant general oversight, both of churches and ministers, is *agreeable* to the *apostolical practice*   But that the office and authority of the apostolate itself have been transmitted, by divine appointment, to any order of men since the apostles, we affirm to be a mere assumption, unsupported by any thing *in* Scripture, or that can be logically inferred from it.

Dr. O takes great pains to prove, what I apprehend no one denies, that there was originally a sacred office, viz, that of the *apostles*, superior to that of elders or presbyters , '' and this [he adds] is substantiating nearly the whole episcopal claim ''*

Is it possible, then, that this is the amount of what Dr O has been labouring through sixteen pages to accomplish? Why, if he had simply stated this proposition at the outset, it would, I presume, have been universally admitted; at least it certainly would by *us*. And yet it is so far from '' substantiating nearly the whole episcopal claim,'' of those who arrogantly assert that they occupy now, by divine right and title, the identical office which the apostles did while on earth in the age of inspiration, that it is not even a single hair's breadth advance toward it   So far as *Scripture testimony alone* is concerned, (and in the argument *now* before us nothing else can be admitted,) the theory that those now called bishops are successors, by divine appointment, to the apostolate itself, as it was held and exercised by the apostles personally in their lifetime, under a direct commission from the Lord Jesus in person, is a mere barefaced hypothesis, an utterly gratuitous assumption, against taking which for granted '' all sound reasoning protests ''   That the establishment of this high '' episcopal claim,'' on the part of himself and others, is, however, absolutely essential to Dr. O 's argument, if he do

* Page 16.

not mean to trifle with his readers, is perfectly manifest: and yet how is he to make it out from *Scripture*, and Scripture *alone?* To any one acquainted with Scripture is it not as plain as the brightest shining of the mid-day sun, that it is impossible to do it? and that Dr O has therefore undertaken an absolutely impossible task?

In preparing for the above conclusion, Dr O seems solicitous to enlarge the original college of apostles by embracing within it several, who, strictly speaking, in regard to the *thing*, the primary apostolate, distinctively understood, have no title to be placed in that rank . In a former part of his essay, indeed, when it seemed sub-servient to *his* purpose, he was careful and ready enough to insist that "irregularity in titles and desig-nations is of so frequent occurrence. yet occasions so little actual confusion, that it ought not to be viewed as a real difficulty in the case before us.* Exactly so, say we, in the present instance It is the *thing* we seek,— the proper, distinctive, original apostolate,—not the mere *name* apostle,—which Dr O. undoubtedly knows is variously used in Scripture, and sometimes in its simple etymological sense, to signify a mere *messenger* on any occasion or mission whatever. Thus St. Paul says to the Philippians, (ii, 25,) that Epaphroditus, their *messenger*, [Gr. Αποστολον, apostle,] had ministered to his wants Examples need not be multiplied , as it is believed that no intelligent and candid reader of the New Testament, both in the Greek and English, will dispute that this term is sometimes used there in its lower, common sense Yet, as Dr O himself well re-marks of some other *names*, "this confusion is but appa-rent, there is no real or practical difficulty" in the case ; a familiar acquaintance with the Scriptures, with even a moderate degree of attention and care, will enable almost any reader to distinguish readily the proper

* Page 12

apostolical office, in its highest distinctive sense, independently of mere *names*

When Dr O argues, therefore, that " the apostles were not thus distinguished because they were appointed by Christ personally , for some are named ' apostles' in Scripture who were not thus appointed, as Matthias, Barnabas, and probably James the brother of the Lord, all ordained by merely human ordainers Silvanus also, and Timothy, and besides Andronicus and Junia others could be added," he evidently violates the just principle by which he wishes to restrict opponents, and argues from the mere *name*, without due regard to the proper distinctions of *things*

With regard to Matthias, in what manner Dr O. would make out that he was not appointed by Christ personally, but was "ordained by merely human ordainers," does not appear   He gives us barely his own assertion for it; which cannot be admitted as *Scripture evidence*   The testimony of that record, on the contrary, is, that previously to the day of Pentecost, when the vacancy in the apostolate occasioned by the apostacy and death of Judas was to be filled, Peter stood up, and after an introductory statement, said, "Wherefore of these men which have companied with us all the time that the Lord Jesus went in and out among us, beginning from the baptism of John, unto that same day that he was taken up from us, must one be ordained to be a witness with us of his resurrection   And they appointed two, Joseph called Barsabas, who was surnamed Justus, and Matthias.   And they prayed, and said, Thou, Lord, which knowest the hearts of all men, show whether of these two thou hast chosen, that he may take part of this ministry and apostleship, from which Judas by transgression fell, that he might go to his own place And they gave forth their lots, and the lot fell upon Matthias, and he was numbered with the eleven apostles,"*

* Acts 1, 21–26

The word "ordained," in the 22d verse of the above passage, may possibly mislead such readers as are not able to examine the passage in the original Greek. Such as are able to do so, however, will be convinced, I am persuaded, by a moment's inspection, that there is no word there in the Greek which can with any propriety be rendered "ordained," in the present ordinary acceptation of the term The words in the Greek, as constructively connected in the 21st and 22d verses, are Δει γενεσθαι,—*must be* That any ecclesiastical rite, "by mere human ordainers," such as imposition of hands, &c, was used on that occasion in the appointment of Matthias to fill the vacancy in the apostolate, there is not one single particle of evidence On the contrary, after Peter's express mention of the Lord Jesus in a preceding verse, the inspired record continues, "And they prayed and said, Thou, Lord, which knowest the hearts of all, show whether of these two THOU *hast chosen,* that he may take part of this ministry and apostleship, . . . and they gave forth their lots, and the lot fell upon Matthias, and he was numbered with the eleven apostles."—obviously (if we take this record alone for our guide, as in this argument we must,) without any farther ceremony, or the interposition of any "mere human ordainers" about it The case was referred, for that peculiar extraordinary office, to the direct personal appointment of the Lord Jesus himself. This Matthias had, in common with the other eleven who then composed the apostolic college. That it was signified by "the lot" does not at all alter the case; for whatever was the specific mode of that lot, of which the record does not inform us, it is plain on the face of the account that the apostles referred its result to the infallible decision of the Lord himself, and that *they believed* that HE HIMSELF did so decide that result; and therefore, without another word or farther act on the subject, according to the record, Matthias "was numbered with the eleven apostles."

Should Dr. O., however, persist in insisting that Matthias was ordained to the apostolate "by mere human ordainers," it seems to me that he will inevitably involve himself in the heresy of *lay* ordination, even to the very highest ecclesiastical office. For let any plain, unbiased reader carefully examine the whole account, and we will cheerfully submit it to his judgment whether, whatever of mere human agency there was in the ordination of Matthias to that office, it was not, so far as the record gives us any information participated in by the whole of the one hundred and twenty disciples.

In regard to Barnabas, there is by no means clear evidence that he was an apostle, in the highest sense of this term, as the twelve and Paul were. The contrary opinion is held by eminent critics, and seems the more probable one. From a case so doubtful, therefore, nothing can be inferred with certainty. The manner in which Dr. O. himself says, " probably James the brother of the Lord," shows his own uncertainty as to the identity of this person, or the propriety of placing him in this class; and it will therefore be as useless as it is unnecessary to discuss the question respecting him, on which the most eminent critics are so much at variance.

But why need I go through the list, since Dr. O. obviously takes advantage merely of the *name* without regard to the *thing* implied in the apostolical office in its distinctive and highest sense. As to Andronicus and Junia, it is very doubtful whether they were ever *named* apostles in any sense. Rom. xvi, 7, is, to say the least, a very doubtful passage as to that point. Junia may even have been the name of a *woman*, the wife of Andronicus, for συγγενεις, rendered *kinsmen* in our version, signifies *relatives* in general, whether male or female. And that they were " of note among the apostles," most probably means nothing more than that they were highly esteemed by them

Silas was a chief man ' among the brethren," and " a faithful brother," as Peter supposed * And that Timothy was subject to the directions of St. Paul, and officially inferior to him, is too plain to be disputed.   To attempt, therefore, as Dr O does, to class among "apostles," distinctively and properly so called, persons whom he alleges to have been "ordained by mere human ordainers," for the sake of establishing the position that those now called bishops occupy by divine right the same office, is to exalt the episcopate at the expense of the apostolate, and thereby, just in the same proportion as this is done, to diminish the credit and the authority of Christianity itself.

The following observations on this subject from the pen of Dr Campbell, are so much in point that I submit them entire to the consideration of the reader —

"Many, indeed, convinced ... that it is in vain to search for the office of bishop, as the word is understood by moderns, in those ministers ordained by the apostles in the churches which they founded, have referred us for its origin to the apostolate itself   I have passingly observed already that this was one of those extraordinary offices which were in their nature temporary, and did not admit succession.   But this point, as so much stress is laid upon it, will deserve to be examined more particularly

" The apostles may be considered in a twofold view,— either in their general character as the first pastors of the church and teachers of the Christian faith, or in what is implied in their special character of apostles of Jesus Christ   In the first general view they are doubtless the predecessors of all those who, to the end of the world, shall preach the same gospel and administer the same sacraments, by whatever name we distinguish them, bishops, priests, or deacons,—overseers, elders, or ministers   But the question still recurs, whether, agreeably to the primitive institution, their successors, in respect of the more common character of teachers and directors of the churches, should be divided into three orders or only into two?   To presume, without evidence, that the first and not the second was the fact, is merely what logicians call a *petitio principii*, taking that for granted which is the very point in dispute But if it be alleged, that not in the general character of teachers, but in their special function as apostles, the bishops are their proper successors, the presbyters and deacons being only the successors of those who were in the beginning ordained by the apostles, this point will require a separate discussion   And for this purpose your attention is entreated to the following remarks

"First, the indispensable requisites in an apostle sufficiently demonstrate that the office could be but temporary   It was necessary that he should be one who had seen Jesus Christ in the flesh after his resurrection. Accordingly they were all especially destined to serve as eye-witnesses to this world of this great event, the hinge on which the truth of Christianity depended The character of apostle is briefly described by Peter, who was himself the first of the apostolical college, as one ordained to be a witness of Christ's resurrection, Acts i, 22 ; a circumstance of which he often makes mention in his speeches, both to the rulers and to the people   See Acts ii, 32 , iii, 15; v, 32; x, 41 , xiii, 31.   And if so, the office, from its nature and design, could not have an existence after the extinction of that generation

"Secondly, the apostles were distinguished by prerogatives which did not descend to any after them.   Of this kind was, first, their receiving their mission immediately from the Lord Jesus Christ, not mediately through any human ordination or appointment · of this kind, also, was, secondly, the power of conferring, by imposition of hands, the miraculous gifts of the Spirit on whomsoever they would , and, thirdly, the knowledge they had, by inspiration, of the whole doctrine of Christ It was for this reason they were commanded to wait the fulfilment of the promise which their Master had given them, that they should be baptized with the Holy Ghost What pains does not Paul take to show that the above-mentioned marks of an apostle belonged to him as well as to any of them! That he had seen Christ after his resurrection, and was consequently qualified, as an eyewitness, to attest that memorable event, he observes, 1 Cor ix, 1 ; xv, 8 , that his commission came directly from Jesus Christ and God the Father, without the intervention of any human creature, he acquaints us, Gal. i, 1 ; ii, 6 To his conferring miraculous powers as the signs of an apostle, he alludes, 2 Cor. xii, 12 , and that he received the knowledge of the gospel, not from any other apostle, but by immediate inspiration, Gal. i, 11, &c

" Thirdly, their mission was of quite a different kind from that of any ordinary pastor It was to propagate the gospel throughout the world, both among Jews and Pagans, and not to take charge of a particular flock. The terms of their commission are, ' Go and teach all nations ;' again, ' Go ye into all the world, and preach the gospel to every creature.' No doubt they may be styled bishops or overseers, but in a sense very different from that in which it is applied to the inspector over the inhabitants of a particular district They were universal bishops , the whole church, or rather the whole earth, was their charge, and they were all colleagues one of another. Or, to give the same sentiment in the words of Chrysostom, Εισιν υπο θεου χειροτονηθεντες αποστολοι αρχοντες, ουκ εθνη και πολεις διαφορους λαμβανοντες, αλλα παντες κοινη την οικουμενην εμπιστευθεντες ' The apostles were constituted of God rulers, not each over a separate nation or city, but all were intrusted with the world in common ' If so, to have limited themselves to any thing less would have been disobedience to the express command they had received from their Master, to go into all nations, and to preach the gospel to every creature If, in the latter part of the lives of any of them, they were, through age and infirmities, confined to one place, that place would naturally fall under the immediate inspection of such And this, if even so much as this, is all that has given rise to the tradition (for there is nothing like historical evidence in the case) that any of them were bishops or pastors of particular churches. Nay, in some instances it is plain that the tradition has originated from this single circumstance, that the first pastors in such a church were appointed by such an apostle Hence it has arisen that the bishops of different churches have claimed (and probably with equal truth) to be the successors of the same apostle

"Fourthly, and lastly. As a full proof that the matter was thus universally understood, both in their own age and in the times immediately succeeding, no one on the death of an apostle was ever substituted in his room , and when that original sacred college was extinct, the title became extinct with it. The election of Matthias by the apostles, in the room of Judas, is no exception, as it was previous to their entering on their charge. They knew it was their Master's intention that twelve missionaries, from among those who had attended his ministry on earth, should be employed as ocular witnesses to attest his resurrection, on which the divinity of his religion depended The words of Peter on this occasion are an ample confirmation of all that has been said, both in regard to the end of the office and the qualifications requisite in the person who fills it, at the same time that they afford a demonstration of the absurdity as well as arrogance of modern pretenders — 'Wherefore of these men which have companied with us all the time that the Lord Jesus went in and out among us, beginning from the baptism of John unto that same day that he was taken up from us, must one be ordained to be a witness with us of his resurrection' But afterward, when the apostle James, the brother of John, was put to death by Herod, as recorded in the Acts of the Apostles, we find no mention made of a successor Nor did the subsequent admission of Paul and Barnabas to the apostleship form any exception to what has been advanced, for they came not as successors to any one, but were especially called by the Holy Spirit as apostles, particularly to the Gentiles, and in them, also, were found the qualifications requisite for the testimony which, as apostles, they were to give "*

The remark of Dr O. that "neither were the apostles thus distinguished because they had seen our Lord after his resurrection, for five hundred brethren saw him,"† is a very singular one. Certainly, it was never meant that all who had thus seen him were therefore apostles, but that none could be apostles who had not thus seen him

Again. he says, "And though the twelve apostles were selected as special witnesses of the resurrection, yet others received that appellation who were not thus selected, as Timothy, Silvanus, Andronicus, Junia, &c,"‡ received *that appellation!* True; as to some at least of those named. But the mere "appellation" is not the *thing* we seek and why does Dr. O thus continue to endeavour to press into his service a mere *name*, against the principle by which he wishes to restrict his opponents The Saviour himself is styled in Scripture "the apostle" of our profession and from his receiving this "appellation," it would seem, according to Dr. O's use of this name in the argument, that, of course, He, and Andronicus, and *Junia* were of the same order, and held identically the same office.

---

* Page 75–78.   † Page 15.   ‡ Ibid.

"Nor were the apostles [he continues] thus distinguished because of their power of working miracles; for Stephen and Philip, who were both deacons, are known to have had this power "* But the apostles had also the farther power of conferring the same gift on others

But why does Dr. O. *separate* the characteristics assigned as distinctive of the apostolate? No one pretends that *any one* of the grounds he names was the sole ground of distinction, as his mode of arguing implies, but that there was a *combination* of the signs of an apostle, to be found in those to whom [the] appellation was appropriate in its highest distinctive sense, and in none else When, therefore, he adds, "It follows, therefore, or will not at least be questioned, that the apostles were distinguished from the elders because they were *superior* to them in ministerial power and rights,"†—if he means, as it would seem he does, that that single circumstance was the whole and sole ground of their entire and peculiar distinction, it is not only "questioned," but flatly denied If, indeed, this notion of Dr O 's be correct, and the matter was so understood by St. Paul and the Corinthian church in his day, is it not surprising that, instead of the course he took to convince them of the legitimateness of his claim to the apostleship, it did not occur to him to say, " Am not I superior to an elder, and therefore, of course, an apostle ?"   *   *   *   *   *
        *   *   *   *   *   *
        *   *   *   *   *   *

* Page 15.   † Ibid.

APPENDIX.

[The remarks embraced in this Appendix appear to have been written separately by the author, with a view of incorporating them afterward in their appropriate places in the Essay. They are added here, because the editor desires to present the subject just as it was left by the author, imperfect as it may be —*Ed*]

I.

The confidence with which Dr. Cooke, though so recent a convert to this high notion, undertakes to unchurch, as it is termed, all those denominations who deny the necessity or the existence, in lineal descent, of the three ministerial orders which he describes as essentially distinct by divine right, may justify a brief inquiry here into the just and Scriptural import of the term " church "

The term itself, as well in the Scriptures and in the writings of the ancient Christian authors as in modern use, has different significations, according to the subject to which it is applied The Greek word generally rendered church in the New Testament is εκκλησια, and signifies either (1,) any civil assemblage of people, lawful or unlawful , or, (2,) when used in reference to the disciples of Christ, the whole Christian community throughout the world , or, (3,) the Christian community in any particular place,—as the church of Jerusalem, of Antioch, &c It has been supposed also by some, in a few passages of Scripture, to signify the place where any Christian society or congregation assembled,—though other able critics doubt this. There are other accommodated significations of the term, which need not be here specified But it may not be amiss to mention that this term is never used in the New Testament in the singular number in reference to Christians, unless when either the church universal is meant, or some particular church in a single place When more than one particular church is intended, but less than the whole, the plural form of the word is always adopted ,—as the churches of Galatia, of Asia, of Macedonia, &c. A national, provincial, or diocesan church, in the singular, as the term is now used, is an application of it altogether unknown in the New Testament, or in the Christian writers of the first two centuries, with the exception of two passages in the epistles attributed to Ignatius, which will be hereafter mentioned In conformity with this statement, one bishop, in the most ancient usage, was uniformly considered as having charge of only one εκκλησια, one church, in the singular ; the extent of which was designated by the Greek word παροικια, in Latin *parochia*, or *paroecia*, which answers to the English word *parish*, and means strictly and properly a *neighbourhood* His charge was never denominated in those early days διοκησις, *a diocese*. This term was not used for this purpose till after the lapse of some centuries, when the bishop's charge had become so far extended as to embrace within it many churches and parishes.

In relation to this subject, Dr C has some singular criticisms on the extent of the church of Jerusalem in the apostolic age, of which I am here reminded —" In Jerusalem,' he says, " there were three thousand persons added to the church on the first day the gospel was publicly preached, after the ascent of our Lord and when Paul went there from Ephesus there was an innumerable company of Christians When he went, on his arrival, to see James, all the presbyters being present, they said unto him, Thou seest how many TENS OF THOUSANDS of Jews there are which believe The words in our translation are, *thou seest how many* THOUSANDS but in the original it is *muriades, myriads, tens of thousands* ." p. 154 Afterward, p 156, assuming as proved what he had before asserted, viz , that these " many myriads,"—even ' *an innumerable company*" of Christians, belonged at that early period to the church in Jerusalem alone,—he adds, " *How many* tens of thousands of believers there were in Jerusalem when Paul went there we cannot exactly say, but it is indisputable that there were *many*, let us suppose *four* only " That is to say, *forty thousand* ONLY, as a moderate calculation, then statedly belonging to the church of Jerusalem alone , for that this is his meaning I take to be plain from the introduction to his criticisms, section 394

But did not the doctor forget that " the multitude" from among whom the three thousand were converted on the day of Pentecost was composed of " Parthians, and Medes, and Elamites, and the dwellers in Mesopotamia, and in Judea, and Cappadocia, in Pontus, and Asia, Phrygia, and Pamphylia, in Egypt, and in the parts of Lybia about Cyrene, and strangers of Rome, Jews and proselytes, Cretes, and Arabians ?" Accordingly, when Peter addressed them, he said, " Ye men of Judea, and all ye that dwell at Jerusalem,—more strictly (οι κατοικουντες) that *sojourn* at Jerusalem,—for a large portion of the hearers, as the context demonstrates, were not inhabitants of *Judea* itself, much less of the city alone They were the strangers mentioned in verses 9, 10, 11, who had come to the feast from the numerous and widely scattered countries there specified Is it reasonable then to suppose that the entire number of the converts was from among the inhabitants of *the city* itself; or that all the converted sojourners continued there afterward, as permanent members of the church of Jerusalem? This is to me, at least, a new idea

He seems to have forgotten, also, that when Paul visited Jerusalem, as stated in the other passage which he cites, (Acts xxi,) it was again during the feast of Pentecost, (as is proved by Acts xx, 16) on which occasion it is well known that a vast concourse of Jews from all quarters, Christians as well as others, who were then still " all zealous of the law," (v 29,) resorted to Jerusalem and, consequently, that the " many myriads" here spoken of can by no principle of rational interpretation be confined to the Jewish believers who were stated inhabitants of Jerusalem alone, but must be understood to include those also who came to the feast from the most distant and various places Indeed the passage Acts xxi, 20, seems to me in all fairness and propriety of construction to include not merely the Jewish believers then present at the feast, from whatever place, but all the Christian believers of that class wherever scattered, who, whether present or not, would undoubtedly hear, through those who were present, of the conduct of Paul , against whom very many of them were already greatly prejudiced

In proof that Dr. C means that there were at that early period so many myriads of Jewish believers inhabitants of Jerusalem, who statedly attended Christian worship there, I need only cite in addition the minute calculation he makes of the size of a building that would contain " forty thousand persons" "in such a parish as Jerusalem," besides "the crowds of unbelievers who continually attended the preaching of the gospel," p 156

This mode of managing the subject reminds me of an argument of Dr. C 's in another place, viz , in that long chain by which he undertakes to establish the episcopate of Timothy at Ephesus   One of the links is, that " only five days elapsed from the time of leaving Troas until the day the elders left Ephesus to go to Miletus, to see Paul "   But how is this proved ? Why simply thus —the distances between certain places are first judged from the map, and it is then presumed,—*in a voyage at sea*, and in the state of navigation at that period,—that equal distances are sailed in equal times, and that for this notable reason, "the general course being the same, *and therefore the wind equally favourable*," p 37   Now had this been a *steamboat* excursion, there might be some tolerable ground for the calculation,—bating accidents   But how " the general course being the same," in a sailboat voyage in the Mediterranean some eighteen hundred years ago, supports the positive conclusion that "*therefore* the wind was equally favourable" for four days successively, I know not   May it not possibly have fallen calm after three days ? or have blown less freshly ? or veered more unfavourably ? or even shifted dead a-head ? Does not the merest fresh-water man know that a distance which in some circumstances may be sailed in a day, in others may require a week, or even a month ? At least one would think this "therefore," in Dr C 's argument, hardly sufficient for one who " had always been in the habit of requiring strong evidence upon every subject, and never yielding assent to any thing" without it , and certainly, rather too weak to constitute any part of a foundation for such a system as he labours to build upon it.   Although, allowing such criticisms and arguments to pass, with what facility *systems may* be reared, it is not difficult to understand

---

II.

The vexed question respecting the original form of government in the Christian church, though not unimportant, is certainly of no such consequence as heated disputants on any side, misled by party prejudices or intemperate zeal, would affect to make it   The declaration of St. Paul that " the kingdom of God is not meat and drink, but righteousness, and peace, and joy in the Holy Ghost," is applicable alike to every thing external and circumstantial , and it may be confidently added, as the apostle continues, " for he that in these things serveth Christ is acceptable to God and approved of men "

But it may be said, perhaps, that this is begging the question , for the ultra high-church, and Dr C among the most forward of that class, in bold, bigoted, often repeated, and extravagant assertions, contends that the form of polity is not a thing external or circumstantial, but of the very essence of a true church   And although no one has ever yet produced, or can produce, a single passage of Scripture which plainly teaches this doctrine,—a thing most marvellous indeed if the doctrine be true ; yet it is urged upon us over and over that *Ignatius* said so, a venerable bishop, father, and martyr, and that we ought to believe him,—especially as his testimony was confirmed too, as Dr C. asserts, by both Polycarp and Irenæus, also venerable fathers, thus making their testimony identical with his , an assertion which shall be examined hereafter   Now, in the first place, we do not believe that Ignatins ever did say so , but that some forger of a later age, and of Dr C 's sentiments, said it for him   And in the second place, if he even did say it, —yet if he or an angel from heaven taught any doctrine different from or inconsistent with the gospel as contained in the New Testament, we would not believe   That Scripture and tradition combined are the source of faith, is the doctrine of Rome, not of Protestants   The doctrine of Protestants is, that the Bible alone is not only the rule, but a sufficient rule, both of faith and practice   Whatever cannot be proved from this, without reference to any other book, or to any tradition, or human authority whatever, Protestants never can consistently receive as an article of faith.   And if Dr C cannot prove without going out of Scripture, that " there is no church" without the three orders of bishops, presbyters, and deacons, as essentially distinct and essentially necessary by Divine appointment , then his argument, Dr Onderdonk being judge, is not "worth taking into account."

Now, that no such thing can be proved *from Scripture*, many of the very ablest writers on the Episcopal side have over and over admitted.   The celebrated Dodwell, the very champion of the highest order of high-church, in the case of the nonjuring bishops in the reign of William III , concedes that all the reasoning from which men conclude that the whole model of ecclesiastical discipline may be extracted from the writings of the New Testament is quite precarious ; that there is no passage of any sacred writer which openly professes this design , that there is not one which so treats of ecclesiastical government as if the writer or the writer's author, the Holy Spirit, had intended to describe any one form of polity as being to remain everywhere and for ever inviolate , that the sacred penmen have nowhere declared with sufficient clearness how great a change must take place in church government, when the churches should first withdraw from the communion of the synagogues, that they nowhere clearly enough show how much was allowed to the personal gifts of the Holy Ghost, and how much also to places and offices, that they nowhere with sufficient accuracy distinguish the extraordinary officers who were [not] to outlive that age, from the ordinary who were not to cease till the second coming of Christ, that all the things then generally known they also suppose known, and never for the sake of posterity explain, minding only the state wherein things were at the time , that they nowhere professedly describe the ministries themselves, so as to explain either their nature or their extent ; which was surely indispensable if they meant to settle a model in perpetuity.*

If all this be so, as every one who reads the Bible can see for himself, " What can we conclude," adds Dr Campbell, " but that it was intended by the Holy Spirit thus to teach us to distinguish between what is essential to the Christian religion, [and to a true church,] and what is comparatively circumstantial, regarding external order and discipline, which, as matters of expedience, alter with circumstances, and are therefore left to the adjustment of human prudence ?   What can better account for the difference remarked by Hoornbeck, that the apostles were more solicitous about the virtues than the degrees of the ministers, and more strenuous in inculcating the manners to be observed by them as suitable to their office, and conducing to their usefulness, than copious in describing the form of their government ?

* I give the entire passage as rendered by Dr George Campbell, Lect on Eccles Hist , pp 52, 53 , where the original Latin of Dodwell may also be seen   And I take pleasure in making a general acknowledgment here, that to Dr Campbell, one of the ablest and most candid critics that I have yet seen on this subject, I am much indebted in various parts of this treatise

12*

The one is essential, the other only circumstantial, the one invariable, the other not."

If the very existence of a church, and the validity of the ministry and ordinances of the gospel, be essentially dependant on the doctrine maintained by Dr Cooke, might we not most reasonably expect to find it so plainly revealed in Scripture that he who runs may read? How else can the perfection of Scripture be asserted? that it is of itself able to make us wise unto salvation,—that the man of God may be perfect, thoroughly furnished unto every good work? And if, moreover, it be alleged to be in Scripture, yet so that even its advocates cannot make it out, confessedly, but by such a precarious chain of far-fetched and subtile deductions as those of Dr Onderdonk, and still more, if, before the chain can possibly be completed, the profound researches of antiquaries, critics, and linguists into the contradictory, the doubtful, and the disputed volumes of the fathers have to be resorted to, does not this of itself afford a strong presumption against it? How, then, may it be said, " *I thank thee, O Father, Lord of heaven and earth, because thou hast hidden these things from the wise and prudent, but hast revealed them unto babes ?*"

According to the doctrine of high-church, when our Lord charged his disciples to " beware of false prophets," he ought to have established a very different criterion by which to judge them. He ought to have taught us how to trace their spiritual pedigree, and how to ascertain whether the pretenders be lineally descended from an apostle or an apostolical bishop, through an unbroken series of prelatical ordinations. Do we find any thing of this sort in Scripture? Is any such thing even intimated or hinted? On the contrary, does not our Lord establish a test entirely different? one of plain, common, and universal application? one suited to the " poor" and ignorant, for whom the gospel with all its immunities and ordinances was specially designed, as well as for the learned. " Ye shall know them by their fruits. Do men gather grapes of thorns, or figs of thistles? Even so every good tree bringeth forth good fruit; but a corrupt tree bringeth forth evil fruit. A good tree cannot bring forth evil fruit, neither can a corrupt tree bring forth good fruit. Wherefore, by their fruits ye shall know them," Matt. vii, 16, 17, 18, 20.

I know that ultra high-churchmen, and Dr C among them, dispute the sufficiency of this test, and attempt a course of argument to disprove it. But then their controversy is with the Master, who expressly affirms and establishes it. And whether we ought to believe him or them, the reader must judge. According to them, Alexander VI, of Rome, and other similar worthies, indispensable links in their chain of succession, were true ministers of Christ, true Christian bishops by Divine appointment, while Francis Asbury, Adam Clarke, Richard Watson, and the brightest luminaries, living or dead, in the Presbyterian, Congregational, Baptist, or Methodist churches, must be held as intruders into the sacred office, and no ministers of Christ. Be it so, by their test. But try them all by the test of Christ, and what will be the result? Surely a writer must calculate largely on the ignorance or the superstition of his readers to talk of establishing such a theory as Dr C's at the present day.

When our blessed Lord, after his resurrection, and just before his ascension, commissioned his apostles to go into all the world, &c., he added, " and lo! I am with you alway, even unto the end of the world." This promise, we are often told, descends to all the true successors of the apostles in the gospel ministry, and to none else. It is granted; and by this test also we are willing to be tried The personal presence of Christ in the flesh, or his presence in miraculous gifts and works, I suppose is not now pretended by any Protestants It remains then that the promise is to be understood of his spiritual presence in the personal support and comfort of his ministers, and in giving sanction and success to their efforts for the conversion and salvation of sinful men by the demonstrations of his Spirit — Are the prelatical monopolizers of the covenant mercies of God, and the presence of Christ, willing that plain people should try their exclusive claims by this test ?*

"Master," said one of the yet imperfectly instructed apostles to Jesus, " we saw one casting out devils in thy name, and we forbade him, because he followeth not us " Jesus answered, " Forbid him not, for there is no man who shall do a miracle in my name that can lightly speak evil of me For he that is not against us is for us." That contracted spirit of exclusionism which regards the party, the cause of the sect, more than the cause of Christ, is not yet extinct. Let him that readeth understand

St John says, " Beloved, believe not every spirit, but try the spirits whether they are of God, because many false prophets are gone out into the world " But how are we to try them ?—by a learned and critical investigation of the truth of their claim to an uninterrupted lineal descent from the apostles, through a long line of baptisms and ordinations of a specific character ? Do the Scriptures anywhere lay down such a test, or anywhere intimate that such should ever be adopted ? " To the law and to the testimony" then " If they speak not according to this word, it is because there is no light in them " This was the legitimate test under the ancient as well as the present dispensation A very different one is now deemed requisite by some zealous patronizers of an exclusive hierarchy, Popish or Protestant.

That any specific form of church government, or mode of authenticating ministers, is not essential to the being of a church, or to the validity of the Christian ministry and ordinances, I take to be plainly the doctrine of the Church of England, if her 23d article be not framed in language designedly ambiguous and deceptive, which ought not to be supposed That article entitled, *Of Ministering in the Congregation*, says, " Those we ought to judge lawfully called and sent, which be chosen and called to this work by men who have public authority given unto them in the congregation to call and send ministers into the Lord's vineyard " This, says Dr Campbell, if it mean any thing, and be not a mere identical proposition, of which he owns it has some appearance, refers us ultimately to that authority, however modelled, which satisfies the people, and is settled among them.

The Episcopal Reformed Church of Scotland, the predecessors of the high-church nonjurors in that country, in their 19th article, entitled, *Of the Notes of the true Kirk*, affirmed that " they [the notes or marks of the

---

* It is related of the late venerable Dr Pilmoor, of Philadelphia, that, after he had become a minister of the Protestant Episcopal Church, he was in a large mixed company, among whom were some of his old friends of the Methodist Episcopal Church, rather tauntingly indulging himself in self gratulation on the above cited promise of Christ's presence with his ministers of the regular apostolical succession, of which he had now the happiness to be one An old friend, who had often heard him preach in the demonstration of the Spirit and of power, when he was a plain Methodist preacher, said to him — " Dr P, permit me to ask you one question, as a candid Christian man When I heard you, as a Methodist preacher, preach to the multitude on the race-ground, the judges' stand being your pulpit, was Christ with you or not ?" The doctor paused, and then emphatically answered, " Yes, if ever he has been with me, he was with me then " His old friend was satisfied, and so were the company It was the candid confession of a plain, honest man,—which plain, honest men knew how to appreciate

true church] are neither antiquity, title usurped, *lineal descent*, place appointed, nor multitude of men approving an error " Again, article 23d, *Of the right Administration of the Sacraments*.—" that sacraments be rightly ministrate, we judge two things requisite the one that they be ministrate by lawful ministers, whom we affirm to be only they that are appointed to the preaching of the word, they being men lawfully chosen thereto by some kirk, &c. We fly the doctrine of the papistical kirk in participation of their sacraments,—1st, Because their ministers are no ministers of Christ Jesus," &c.   Here, continues Dr Campbell, not only is lineal descent expressly excluded, but its very channel is removed, as the Popish clergy are declared (he thinks with too little ceremony and too universally) to be no ministers of Christ   Nay, all that appears externally necessary, according to that episcopal formulary, to constitute a minister, is the choice of some congregation   Far from believing one particular form of ecclesiastical polity to be sacred and inviolable, they say, Art. 21, *Of General Councils, &c.*, " Not that we think any policy and any order of ceremonies can be appointed for all ages, times, and places "

Dr Cooke is careful frequently to remind us that some of the ancient authors on whom he relies were martyrs.   Is nothing due then to the testimony of the venerable martyrs of that mother church from which his own recently adopted communion claims birth ?   What was the language of Rogers, who, though with a wife and ten children, whom he was not even suffered to see, refused a pardon at the stake from those successors of the apostles and vicegerents of Christ, the then bishops of England ?   What was the language of Bishop Hooper, whom the popish bishops, Christ's true and supreme ministers by Divine appointment, according to Dr C., brought also to the stake ? and who was used so barbarously in the fire, that his legs and thighs were roasted, and one of his hands dropped off, before he expired,—a man not inferior to Ignatius himself in piety, or in sufferings for Christ ? When brought before their prelatical judges, they were asked whether they would submit to the church or not   But they answered that they looked on the church of Rome as *antichristian* *   Bishop Hooper, in particular, while in prison, and about two months before his martyrdom, wrote a letter dated December 11, 1554, in which are these expressions —" With us [in England] the wound which Antichrist [the pope or the popish church] had received is healed, and he [the pope] is declared head of the church, *who is not a member of it* "† How little idea had this venerable episcopal martyr of the English church that his own ministerial and episcopal character depended wholly on a spiritual pedigree which could be traced in a direct line to what he believed to be " Antichrist !"

It is granted that, for the sake of discipline and order in the settlement of churches, it is proper to limit the power of administering the sacraments of baptism and the Lord's supper to fewer hands than preaching   But if it be required to make up and pronounce *from Scripture* a candid judgment of what is *valid* in cases of exigence, or what is essential to the being of a church, then can it be doubted that even any private Christian was warranted in the apostolical age, and is still if he can, to convert a sinner from the error of his ways, and to teach him the principles of the Christian faith ? Yet were not these two important parts of the apostolical commission ?—

* Burnet's Hist., [Abridgment] vol. ii, p. 272
† Neal's Hist. of the Puritans, vol. i, p. 139.

Would it be amiss to say that they were even the most important ? Our Lord himself made proselytes and instructed them, but baptized none,—leaving this merely ministerial work to his disciples. Peter was sent to open the door of faith to Cornelius and his family, but the charge of baptizing them he intrusted entirely to the Christian brethren who attended him Ananias, a disciple, was employed to baptize Paul And Paul says himself of his own mission, that Christ sent him not to baptize, but to preach the gospel, denoting thereby that baptizing, compared with preaching, though a part, was but an inferior and subordinate part, of his charge *

In the epistles attributed to Ignatius, the phrase " *the church which is in Syria*" occurs twice   This, Dr Campbell thinks, has much the appearance of an anachronism, which often betrays the hand of the interpolator Nothing, he observes, can be more dissimilar to the dialect which prevailed in the apostolic age, and which continued to prevail in the second century   Except when *the church* denoted the whole Christian community, it meant no more than a single congregation   When, through the increase of converts, a bishop's parish, indeed, came to contain more people than could be contained in one congregation, the custom continued of still calling his charge *a church*, in the singular number   But it was not till after the distinction made between the metropolitan and the suffragans, which was about a century later, that this use originated of calling all the churches of a province the church (not the churches) of such a province   After the rise of the patriarchal jurisdiction the application of the term was extended still farther   All that was under the jurisdiction of the archbishop as patriarch was his church †

That the early fathers entertained no such ideas of the essential characteristics of a Christian church, as Dr Cooke has asserted, out of Ignatius, is plain from a striking passage in Tertullian who, in the beginning of the third century, explicitly asserted that " *three persons, though laymen, make a church*" His words are, " *Sed ubi tres, ecclesia est, licet laici* " referring in the same place to a known practice even down to his time, viz , that when none of the clerical order could be had, (that is to say, in the exigence of necessity,) even private Christians celebrated the eucharist, and baptized, and served as priests to themselves " *Ubi ecclesiastici ordinis non est consessus, et offers, et tinguis, et sacerdos es tibi solus* "

Any person acquainted with the Latin language, and a stranger to the later disputes about sacerdotal orders, would hardly conceive the passage quoted from Tertullian susceptible of any other interpretation than that above given   Yet pains have been taken by persons who, as Dr Campbell observes, cannot conceive a kingdom of Christ that is not a kingdom of priests, totally to disguise it   Tertullian's argument, in the place cited, obviously is, that in case of necessity even laymen have the right of priesthood in themselves ; and this argument he confirms by the reference above mentioned to the known and uncensured practice of his time   The argument in this view was to his purpose, in any other it was utterly futile —By the way, this passage serves also to show how widely different were the views of Tertullian and the Christian church of that age, from those now entertained and asserted by Dr Onderdonk, in regard to the Christian sacraments in exigences of necessity

* See Campbell, Eccles Hist , pp 62, 63
† Ibid , pp 100, 101

That these principles are sanctioned by the earliest practice of the Christian church in the apostolical age, may be deduced from the testimony of Hilary, also a distinguished deacon of the Church of Rome, in the fourth century, who openly and without censure asserted that " Postquam omnibus locis ecclesiæ sunt constitutæ, et officia ordinata, aliter composita res est, quam cœperat, primum enim omnes docebant, et omnes baptizabant, quibuscunque diebus vel temporibus fuisset occasio " " Ut ergo cresceret plebs, et multiplicaretur, omnibus inter initia concessum est et evangelizare, et baptizare, et scripturas in ecclesia explanare " Comm on Eph iv. [" After churches were established in every place, and offices ordained, things were managed otherwise than at the beginning for, at first, all used to teach, and all to baptize, on whatever days or seasons there might be occasion "— " That the people might increase and be multiplied, it was at first granted to all to preach the gospel, and to baptize, and to explain the Scriptures in the church."—*Ed.*]

I do not say that this is proper where there are organized churches and regular pastors , but that, when there are not, in circumstances corresponding in effect to those of the primitive church at the period alluded to, the principle is still the same , and that, consequently, there is nothing in the principles of the gospel, or the allowed practice of the apostolical age, making it unlawful, but, on the contrary, much to justify it   This was manifestly the opinion of the Christians who, " except the apostles," were scattered abroad in consequence of the persecution which arose against the church in Jerusalem at the time of Stephen's martyrdom   for they " went everywhere preaching the word "   The apostles, it will be observed, remained in Jerusalem   All the rest went everywhere preaching the word and yet there is not the slightest intimation in the history that the apostles, though so recently commissioned directly by their Lord, denounced this course, or manifested any such spirit of exclusiveness as high-church bigots now exhibit.

[THE END.]

Date Due

CPSIA information can be obtained at www.ICGtesting.com
Printed in the USA
BVOW052007100613

322941BV00003B/43/P

9 781178 567243